T0140921

Behavioral and Neural Mechanisms Underlying Dynamic Face Perception

Dissertation

zur Erlangung des Grades eines
Doktors der Naturwissenschaften

der Mathematisch-Naturwissenschaftlichen Fakultät
und
der Medizinischen Fakultät
der Eberhard-Karls-Universität Tübingen

vorgelegt

von

Katharina Dobs

aus Frankfurt am Main

Juni 2014

Bibliografische Information der Deutschen Nationalbibliothek

Die Deutsche Nationalbibliothek verzeichnet diese Publikation in der
Deutschen Nationalbibliografie; detaillierte bibliografische Daten sind
im Internet über http://dnb.d-nb.de abrufbar.

ISBN 978-3-8325-3910-8

Logos Verlag Berlin GmbH
Comeniushof, Gubener Str. 47,
10243 Berlin
Tel.: +49 (0)30 42 85 10 90
Fax: +49 (0)30 42 85 10 92
INTERNET: http://www.logos-verlag.de

Tag der mündlichen Prüfung: 17. Dezember 2014

Dekan der Math.-Nat. Fakultät: Prof. Dr. W. Rosenstiel
Dekan der Medizinischen Fakultät: Prof. Dr. I. B. Autenrieth

1. Berichterstatter: Prof. Dr. Heinrich H. Bülthoff
2. Berichterstatter: Prof. Dr. Martin A. Giese

Prüfungskommission: Prof. Dr. Heinrich H. Bülthoff
                                    Prof. Dr. Martin A. Giese
                                    Andreas Bartels, Ph.D.
                                    Betty Mohler, Ph.D.

Acknowledgements

I would like to thank my supervisors Dr. Isabelle Bülthoff and Dr. Johannes Schultz for the supervision of this work, their great support and steady encouragement, Prof. Heinrich H. Bülthoff for his support and the promotion of my PhD, and the members of my advisory board, Prof. Dr. Michael J. Black, Prof. Dr. Martin A. Giese and Dr. Quoc C. Vuong for their help and constructive criticism. Further, I would like to thank Dr. Justin L. Gardner for the supervision and fruitful discussions during and after my time at the RIKEN Brain Science Institute.

I thank Dr. Martin Breidt and Dr. Cristóbal Curio for technical advice on creating my stimuli, and I am especially thankful to Mario Kleiner for his support with the motion-retargeting system and to Dr. Stephan de la Rosa for his advices on statistics. Further, I thank my colleagues, in particular the members of RECCAT, for an inspiring and delightful time.

I am also grateful to my family for their support and encouragement. Most of all I would like to thank Markus who fills my life with love, happiness and adventures.

Abstract

Dynamic faces are highly complex, ecologically and socially relevant stimuli which we encounter almost every day. How the face perception system extracts information from this rich source is still far from understood. The current thesis investigates how the extraction of different kinds of information conveyed by dynamic faces is coordinated.

Part I comprises of two psychophysical experiments examining the mechanisms underlying facial motion processing. Facial motion can be represented as high-dimensional spatio-temporal data defining how the face is moving over time. Previous studies suggest that these spatio-temporal data can be adequately synthesized by using simple approximations to investigate human face perception. In the first experiment, we argue against the use of synthetic facial motion by showing that the human face perception system is highly sensitive towards manipulations of the natural spatio-temporal characteristics of facial motion. In the second experiment, we further show that facial motion, when performed in unconstrained contexts, helps identity judgments. Thus, two mechanisms underlying the coordination of facial motion processing are proposed: first, a transformation of visual input into a sparse but meaningful spatio-temporal code representing facial motion; second, a mechanism that extracts identity information from this spatio-temporal code.

Part II presents a functional magnetic resonance imaging (fMRI) study investigating the neural processing of expression and identity information in dynamic faces. Previous studies proposed a distributed neural system for face perception which distinguishes between invariant (e.g., identity) and changeable (e.g., expression) aspects of faces. Attention is a potential candidate mechanism to coordinate the processing of these two facial features. Two findings are presented that support this hypothesis: first, attention to expression versus identity of dynamic faces dissociates cortical areas assumed to process changeable aspects from those involved in discriminating invariant aspects of faces; second, attention leads to a more precise neural representation of the attended facial feature. Further, the superior temporal sulcus represented both expression and identity, while a part of the inferior occipital gyrus represented identity irrespective of the attended feature; these findings gave rise to the hypothesis that interactions between identity and expression information may be mediated by those areas.

Content

1 Synopsis

1.1 Why are dynamic faces interesting?

Most of the faces we encounter and interact with everyday move - when we meet a friend, we express continuous facial movements such as nodding, smiling and speaking. These facial movements can be categorized into rigid head motion (e.g., as in nodding) and non-rigid facial motion (e.g., in a smiling expression, or speech movements). From the information conveyed by facial motion we can extract various cues about the friend's state of mind, such as her affective state or the intensity of her emotions. Further, in a noisy environment, the conversation becomes more intelligible when perceiving the movements of her mouth, while the rigid movement of her head indicates her focus of attention.

It is quite astonishing how quickly and seemingly effortlessly we can process the vast amount information conveyed by dynamic faces. However, much of this information, such as sex, age or basic expressions like anger, can even be recognized from only a brief glance at a static image of the face. If we can perceive and recognize much from static faces alone, what details do we additionally extract from the spatio-temporal characteristics of facial motion? Is it even necessary to use natural facial movements as stimuli to investigate facial motion processing, or would simple approximations be sufficient? Indeed, compared to static faces, natural facial motion carries additional information about facial speech (Bernstein, Tucker, & Demorest, 2000; Rosenblum et al., 2002) and expressions, particularly for expressions that are more complex than the classic basic emotions (Ambadar, Schooler, & Cohn, 2005; Cunningham & Wallraven, 2009; Kaulard, Cunningham, Bülthoff, & Wallraven, 2012). Despite these findings, it is still unclear which cues we specifically extract from the rich and complex spatio-temporal characteristics of facial motion.

Beside these rich communication signals that are conveyed by facial motion, it seems reasonable to ask whether facial motion might also be a cue to the identity of a person. For example, when an impersonator mimics a famous person's facial expressions, we are able to recognize this person. In line with this observation, studies suggest that facial motion contains idiosyncratic movements which can provide a cue to the person's identity (Hill & Johnston, 2001; Knappmeyer, Thornton, & Bülthoff, 2003;

Lander & Bruce, 2003; Lander & Chuang, 2005; O'Toole, Roark, & Abdi, 2002). Yet, it is still unclear which facial movements contain identity information and how efficiently our face perception system extracts identity information from these facial movements (O'Toole et al., 2002). Do we express more identity information in our facial movements when we are in a conversation with someone compared to when we are angry?

As mentioned above, dynamic faces convey at least two major sources of information relevant for our daily social interactions: information about the identity and the expression of a face. When seeing a friend, we may need to extract identity information from his face to recognize him and information about his facial expression to interpret his mood. Moreover, as has been demonstrated in the impersonator example given above, we can recognize a famous person's facial movements although the impersonator's facial shape and texture may be quite different from the person. The fact that we can disentangle facial motion from facial form information raises another question: How does our brain represent and selectively extract information about these two socially relevant cues? In other words, if we can recognize someone by his facial movements being mimicked on a different face (e.g., the impersonator's), are facial form and facial motion processed separately and how much do these features interact during processing of dynamic faces?

In summary, dynamic faces are information-rich and ecologically salient stimuli that are of importance for a number of social tasks. In particular, facial motion might carry cues to identity in addition to the facial form of a face and might be used to recognize a person. However, how we process dynamic faces remains open and the exact mechanisms still need to be unraveled. Thus, the investigation of dynamic face processing with methods that allow control for motion and identity information can advance our understanding of how we perceive faces in real life.

The current thesis presents a range of experiments that aim at addressing the open questions introduced above. All experiments used facial animations based on natural facial motion as dynamic face stimuli. Specifically, two psychophysical experiments, presented in Chapters 2 and 3, examine the sensitivity to natural facial motion and identity information in dynamic faces, respectively. A functional magnetic resonance imaging (fMRI) experiment investigating the neural representation of identity and expression of dynamic faces is presented in Chapter 4. An overview and discussion of the experiments can be found in section 1.5 of this chapter. After a brief overview of common techniques to investigate facial motion (section 1.2), the remainder of this chapter makes the reader acquainted with the major theoretical and neural models that are of importance to study face perception in general (section 1.3), and identity information in dynamic faces in particular (section 1.4).

1.2 How to study facial motion?

Traditionally, face perception research has focused on static stimuli, such as photographs of human faces to investigate face processing. It is only recently that dynamic faces have been used as stimuli to study faces in a more ecological setting. Table 1 gives a schematic overview of the most common types of stimuli used to investigate facial motion perception. Early studies mostly used video recordings of faces as stimuli to investigate facial motion processing (see first row in Table 1). While viewing movies of faces capture much of the visual experience of perceiving real-life faces, it is difficult to assess the content of information in such natural stimuli, let alone to parametrically control this information.

One way to achieve this control is to use point-light face stimuli, in which only reflective markers attached to the surface of a moving face are visible (Atkinson, Vuong, & Smithson, 2012; Bassili, 1978; Berry, 1991; Pollick, Hill, Calder, & Paterson, 2003). However, point-light stimuli are highly degraded and unnatural. To address the trade-off between naturalness (e.g., movies of faces) and a high degree of control (e.g., point-light faces), an increasing number of studies use synthetic faces as stimuli and animate them based on spatio-temporal properties of facial expressions (Hill & Johnston, 2001; Knappmeyer et al., 2003; Ku et al., 2005). The naturalness of these stimuli might vary from unnatural to natural depending on the quality of the synthetic faces as well as the motion information used to animate these faces.

One way to animate synthetic faces based on natural facial motion is to use recorded motion data from actors performing different facial expressions and directly map these to synthetic faces (Cook, Matei, & Johnston, 2011; Knappmeyer et al., 2003; Walder, Breidt, Bülthoff, Schölkopf, & Curio, 2009). While the resulting facial animations provide a close approximation of natural facial expressions, it is still technically challenging and time consuming to systematically manipulate the underlying temporal characteristics of the motion-capture data.

3

To address this challenge, complex and detailed facial movements can be created with a commonly used coding scheme for facial motion called Facial Action Coding System (FACS; Ekman, Friesen, & Hager, 2002; Ekman & Friesen, 1978). This system uses a number of discrete 'face movements' - termed Action Units - as an intuitive and accurate description of the basic constituents of most facial expressions, static or dynamic. Importantly, the temporal characteristics of each Action Unit can be semantically described (e.g., as eyebrow raising) and can be modified quantitatively and separately to induce systematic *local* changes in the facial motion (Jack, Garrod, Yu, Caldara, & Schyns, 2012; Yu, Garrod, & Schyns, 2012). A recent line of facial animation approaches have synthesized time courses of the Action Units in FACS to approximate facial expressions in the absence of actor data (Roesch et al., 2010; Yu et al., 2012). For example, Yu et al. (2012) interpolated the time courses for each Action Unit based on three randomly selected 'control points' – represented as point in time and activation magnitude. However, this method is restricted to those parameters and not based on natural, recorded face motion data.

Alternatively, Curio et al. (2006) developed a novel 3D facial animation approach to automatically decompose natural facial motion-capture data into local facial movements - termed facial actions - and render them as synthetic facial expressions in a space similar to FACS with semantically meaningful facial actions. The authors validated their system by showing that using a set of local facial actions to approximate facial motion led to more natural animations than using a global approximation of the compound peak expression. Importantly, facial animations rendered by this system are based on natural facial motion but allow for meaningful interpretation of the underlying motion characteristics, for quantification as well as for systematic manipulation of the rich information in dynamic faces.

Table 1. Schematic overview of common techniques used to investigate facial motion processing.

	Naturalness	Control	Technical Demand	Example
Movies	high	low	low	
Point-light faces	low	high	medium	
Facial animation	low to high	high	high	

We decided to use facial animations as stimuli for the experiments presented in the current thesis based on the system introduced by Curio et al. (2006). A detailed explanation of our facial animation procedure can be found in Appendix 1 of Chapter 2. Briefly, we captured facial movements of non-professional female actors using a commercial motion capture system. The facial marker positions were tracked by infra-red cameras, while an additional camera recorded a video of the actor performing the facial movements (see Figure 1). At the beginning of each motion capture session, various facial actions (e.g., eyebrow raising) were captured from the actor (see Table A.1 in Chapter 2). Each actor then performed different facial movements occurring in various social contexts (e.g., anger or 'speak angrily to someone'). The non-rigid parts of facial motion capture data were post-processed and decomposed into time courses of facial actions. These time courses were then used to animate a female 3D head model to produce our facial animation stimuli.

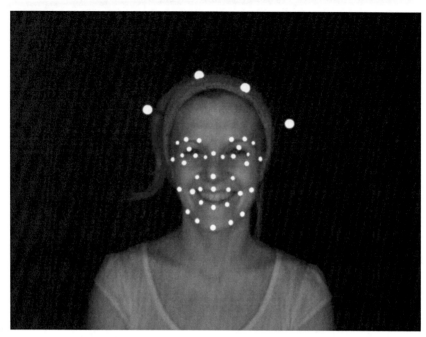

Figure 1. Exemplary frame of a video recorded by the scene camera during motion capture. 37 facial markers and four additional markers attached to a headband were tracked by six infra-red cameras.

1.3 Models of face perception

Face perception is based on various aspects of faces - we can perceive a person's identity from the facial structure or the person's affective state using their facial expression. Current models of face perception distinguish between these aspects as invariant (e.g., facial identity) and changeable (e.g., facial expression) aspects of faces which are processed in distinct functional processing routes (Bruce & Young, 1986; Calder & Young, 2005; Haxby, Hoffman, & Gobbini, 2000). In general, it is accepted that many different brain regions are involved in face processing. The core system comprises three areas: the Occipital Face Area (OFA; see Figure 2) in the inferior occipital gyrus (Allison et al., 1994; Gauthier & Logothetis, 2000); the posterior part of the superior temporal sulcus (STS; see Figure 2) (Allison, Puce, & McCarthy, 2000; Narumoto, Okada, Sadato, Fukui, & Yonekura, 2001); and the Fusiform Face Area (FFA; see Figure 2) in the lateral fusiform gyrus (Gauthier & Logothetis, 2000; Kanwisher, McDermott, & Chun, 1997; Sergent, Ohta, & MacDonald, 1992). While OFA is thought to be involved in early perception of facial features (Pitcher, Walsh, & Duchaine, 2011), FFA and STS are thought to process invariant and changeable aspects of faces, respectively (Haxby et al., 2000). Several studies found that ventral temporal face-sensitive regions also respond more to moving than to static faces (Fox, Iaria, & Barton, 2009; Schultz & Pilz, 2009). In a more recent study, Schultz and colleagues showed that the higher activation in these regions was due to the increased amount of static information present in moving faces rather than to the meaningful deformation of the face over time (Schultz, Brockhaus, Bülthoff, & Pilz, 2013). This is consistent with the idea that ventral temporal regions are not involved in processing changeable aspects of faces.

Several lines of evidence support the distributed model of face perception summarized above. Results from behavioral and neuroimaging studies suggested functionally and neuroanatomically dissociable pathways for processing invariant and changeable aspects of faces (e.g., Bruce & Young, 1986; Hoffman & Haxby, 2000; Parry, Young, Shona, & Saul, 1991; Sergent, Ohta, MacDonald, & Zuck, 1994; Winston, Henson, Fine-Goulden, & Dolan, 2004). Furthermore, studies investigating neural correlates of attention found decreased activation in face-processing areas when attention was directed away from faces (Furey et al., 2006; O'Craven, Downing, & Kanwisher, 1999; Wojciulik, Kanwisher, & Driver, 1998). More specifically, functional magnetic resonance imaging (fMRI) studies have suggested that selective attention to changeable versus invariant features of faces specifically increases activity in areas processing the attended features (Hoffman & Haxby, 2000; Narumoto et al., 2001). To date, it is not fully understood why the neural activity in these areas increases with attention, and the underlying mechanisms of this attentional modulation still need to be further investigated.

However, divergent results reporting expression information in FFA (Fairhall & Ishai, 2007; Xu & Biederman, 2010) and facial identity information in parts of STS (Winston et al., 2004) have also been found. Moreover, studies failed to find a double dissociation between facial identity and expression recognition (see Calder & Young, 2005) and, in contrast, revealed asymmetric relationships between the perception of facial identity and expression (Schweinberger & Soukup, 1998; Schweinberger, Burton, & Kelly, 1999). These results suggest a stronger interaction between the two processing pathways than previously assumed. In particular, the role of facial motion in identity processing is still under debate and theoretical accounts will be introduced in the following section.

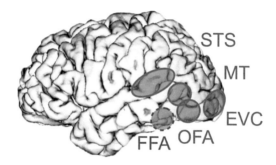

Figure 2. Schematic overview of the cortical areas investigated in this thesis. Areas are shown on the left hemisphere. Early visual processing areas comprise the early visual cortex (EVC), the occipital face area (OFA), and the medial temporal lobe (MT), shown in grey. A posterior part of superior temporal sulcus (STS, shown in blue) is assumed to process changeable aspects, while the fusiform face area (FFA, shown in purple but not directly visible from the lateral perspective) is assumed to process invariant aspects of faces. Schematic brain hemisphere has been redrawn and compiled from Schultz, Brockhaus, Bülthoff, & Pilz, 2013.

1.4 The role of facial motion in identity processing

Two hypotheses about the way facial motion might contribute to person recognition have been put forward (O'Toole et al., 2002). The *supplemental information hypothesis* postulates that idiosyncratic facial motions of individuals are represented in the brain and can be used for identification in addition to form information. The *representation enhancement hypothesis* posits that facial motion influences recognition by facilitating the perception of the three-dimensional structure of a face. The authors assume that the two hypotheses could complement each other. However, there are only few studies indicating that the representation enhancement hypothesis plays an important role in face recognition (Lander & Bruce, 2003).

Evidence from experiments with various designs support the supplemental information hypothesis. Hill and Johnston reported that participants could discriminate identities based on rigid facial motion animated on an average head (Hill & Johnston, 2001). In addition, Knappmeyer and colleagues could show that previously learned non-rigid facial motion characteristics can bias identity decisions (Knappmeyer et al., 2003).

Lander and Chuang found a benefit for facial motion when recognizing people in degraded viewing conditions (Lander & Chuang, 2005). In contrast to the findings of Hill and Johnston, this effect was only advantageous for expressive and talking movements but not for rigid motion. In a follow-up study, Lander et al. (2006) found that the recognition of familiar faces was significantly improved when the faces were shown smiling naturally compared to artificially smiling, i.e. a video created by morphing over time a non-smiling static face into a smiling one (Lander, Chuang, & Wickham, 2006). Lander and colleagues assumed that the recognition advantage for face motion was due to the storage of an individual's characteristic motion in memory and can therefore be distinguished from a general benefit for motion. The results further suggested a rather precise spatio-temporal code of facial motion representation in the brain.

At first sight, the results presented above seem difficult to integrate in the widely accepted neural model of face perception (Haxby et al., 2000). Given that both invariant and changeable aspects of faces are useful for identification, and these aspects are assumed to be processed in distinct pathways, how is the information from both pathways integrated to recognize a moving face? In particular, if facial motion carries expression and identity information, how do we selectively extract one or the other? These questions are particularly relevant as most of the studies supporting the distributed neural model of face perception were based on static faces.

However, recent studies have extended the neural model of face perception to integrate dynamic face processing (Foley, Rippon, Thai, Longe, & Senior, 2012; O'Toole et al., 2002). In particular, two candidate areas which may mediate the interaction between identity and expression information have been put forward: the motion-processing area in middle temporal lobe (MT; (O'Toole et al., 2002) and the face-sensitive area OFA (Foley et al., 2012; Furl, Henson, Friston, & Calder, 2014). In line with the hypothesis that OFA might mediate the interaction between identity and expression, studies using static faces as stimuli found that OFA was sensitive to changes in faces independent of a categorical change in identity or expression (Fox et al., 2009; Rotshtein, Henson, Treves, Driver, & Dolan, 2004), and even independent of awareness of these changes (Large, Cavina-Pratesi, Vilis, & Culham, 2008). Yet, to date, most studies focused on face-sensitive areas and thus the question how earlier visual cortex areas (EVC; see Figure 2) and motion-processing area MT are involved in face perception is still to be investigated.

1.5 Thesis overview and discussion

This thesis consists of two parts, and presents studies investigating the behavioral and neural processing of different aspects of dynamic faces. The aim is to advance our understanding of how the face perception system processes facial motion and form information of dynamic faces.

Part I of the current thesis, which includes Chapter 2 and 3, presents behavioral studies of facial motion processing that address the following two main questions: (1) What cues do we extract from facial motion and how sensitive are we to natural spatio-temporal information in dynamic faces? (2) Which facial movements contain identity information, and how does the face perception system extract this information? These questions are addressed in two psychophysical experiments in human observers that are presented in Chapters 2 and 3, respectively. Part II, which comprises Chapter 4, is related to the neural processing mechanisms underlying dynamic face processing. The aim of the presented human fMRI study is to unravel the cortical mechanisms that allow us to selectively extract information from the facial form and the facial motion of a face. The following sections summarize and discuss these results with respect to the most relevant research.

Part I

Facial motion is a complex stimulus containing several cues, which include idiosyncratic motion (for a review see Roark, Barrett, Spence, Herve, & O'Toole, 2003), the timing and intensity of facial expressions (Jack et al., 2012; Kamachi et al., 2001) and speech movements (Bernstein et al., 2000; Rosenblum et al., 2002). During social interactions, we constantly read and interpret the information conveyed by these cues.

Recently, a series of studies have used synthesized time courses for FACS Action Units to generate animations of facial expressions in the absence of actor data (Jack et al., 2012; Roesch et al., 2010; Yu et al., 2012). Given their simplicity and ease of control, such stimuli have been used in many studies investigating facial motion perception (Furl et al., 2010; Ku et al., 2005; LaBar, Crupain, Voyvodic, & McCarthy, 2003; Sarkheil, Goebel, Schneider, & Mathiak, 2013; Sato & Yoshikawa, 2007). However, it is still unclear whether such simplistic stimuli are perceived as good approximations of natural facial motion dynamics.

Indeed, several studies suggest that observers are sensitive to the timing of local changes in facial motion distributed across the whole face (Curio et al., 2006; Yu et al., 2012). However, none of these studies systematically tested the perceptual effect of artificial facial motion generated with different methods of approximating the time course of each facial action. Thus, two important related questions arise: How sensitive are we to the spatio-temporal profiles of facial motion? And do we perceive differences between artificially created spatio-temporal profiles based on approximation methods and natural profiles based on human-actor data?

In Chapter 2 of this thesis, we investigated how sensitive observers are to natural spatio-temporal information in facial expressions and what cues they extract when making judgments about these movements. Our results revealed observers' sensitivity to changes of natural facial dynamics. Importantly, our method allows a quantitative explanation of the perceived similarity of dynamic facial expressions, which suggests that sparse but meaningful spatio-temporal cues are used to process facial motion.

Why are we highly sensitive to natural facial motion dynamics? We hypothesize that one reason is that spatio-temporal information in facial movements is also used for identity perception. Previous studies have shown that characteristic facial movements may carry cues about identity which humans can use to categorize or recognize persons (Hill & Johnston, 2001; Knappmeyer et al., 2003; Lander et al., 2006; Lander & Chuang, 2005), suggesting a stronger interaction between the processing of facial motion and identity than previously assumed. To date, the exact role of facial motion as a cue for identity is still under debate (O'Toole et al., 2002). In particular, which facial movements are idiosyncratic, and when and how the face perception system extracts identity information from these facial movements, is still unknown.

Chapter 3 examines the role of social context and the type of facial movement on identity judgments from facial motion. We hypothesized that the less stereotypical facial expressions are, the more identity information they would convey. To this end, we tested human observers and compared their identity judgments to the performance of ideal observers based on the spatio-temporal properties of facial motion. Our findings reveal (i) that human observers cannot recognize unfamiliar persons from the way they perform basic emotional facial expressions even though, as revealed by ideal observer analyses, these expressions do contain some identity information, and (ii) that such recognition is possible from conversational and speech-related movements which contain more identity information. We believe that these differences are due to the constraints under which these movements are executed: basic emotions can be performed quite stereotypically, whereas conversational and speech-related movements may be performed more idiosyncratically.

Taken together, our studies show how sensitive our perception of face motion is, and highlights distinct roles of different types of facial movements for face perception. Moreover, thanks to the high degree of stimulus control, our approach will allow us in the future to ask precise questions about how facial motion carries identity information, and how it is processed.

Part II

Part II of this thesis focuses on the cortical mechanisms underlying the processing of facial motion and facial form of dynamic faces. In daily life, we constantly need to extract identity information to recognize a person and information about facial expressions to interpret a person's mood. What are the cortical mechanisms that allow us to selectively extract information about these two important cues? Current models of face perception distinguish between these features as invariant (i.e., facial identity) and changeable (i.e., facial expression) aspects of faces which are predominantly processed in distinct cortical areas (Haxby et al., 2000). In contrast to this theory, many studies have reported expression and identity information across face-sensitive areas (Fox et al., 2009; Nestor, Plaut, & Behrmann, 2011; Winston et al., 2004; Xu & Biederman, 2010) suggesting a stronger interaction between the two facial features than previously assumed. However, it is still unclear which cortical areas may transfer information between areas processing invariant and areas processing changeable aspects of faces.

In Chapter 4 of this thesis, we hypothesize that attention enhances the representation of facial features in the face processing network. That is, we expect an improved representation of identity and expression when attending to these socially relevant facial features. This hypothesis is supported by our experimental results. We conducted an fMRI experiment in which participants attended to either the expression or identity of the same dynamic faces, while their brain activity was measured. We were able to reliably decode which facial feature (i.e., expression or identity) was attended to across multiple cortical areas. These cortical areas could further be dissociated by which feature elicited greater activity. Importantly, the representation of identity and expression were enhanced with attention across multiple cortical areas. Interestingly, area STS represented both identity and expression, while area OFA represented identity irrespective of the attentional task.

Our results are the first to find an enhanced representation of high-level facial features - identity and expression - with attention across multiple stages of the visual face processing system. Thus, they suggest that attention might act as a mechanism to boost the representations of these high-level facial features. Moreover, our results indicate that area OFA might transfer identity information to area STS that processes changeable aspects of faces but represents identity and expression information.

General discussion

The current thesis investigates the behavioral and neural mechanisms underlying dynamic face perception. To systematically study the perception of dynamic faces, highly controllable and accurate animations of facial movements are needed. However, dynamic face information is highly complex, which makes it difficult to isolate and quantify meaningful cues. To address this challenge, we decided to use a system that decomposes recorded motion data into time courses of facial actions (e.g., eyebrow raising) which are used to animate a 3D head model with corresponding facial actions (Curio et al., 2006). Importantly, these facial action time courses are form-independent. That is, the system intrinsically separates facial motion from facial form cues. Moreover, by using this system we could not only render high-quality facial animations based on natural facial motion but we could also quantify and manipulate the spatio-temporal information in these facial animations.

In Chapter 2, we validate the relevance of our stimuli by reporting two major findings: First, the human perceptual system is highly sensitive to degradations of the spatio-temporal properties of natural facial motion. Second, sparse but meaningful spatio-temporal cues are used to represent and process facial motion. These results have important implications for theories of mental representations of facial motion. In particular, they suggest that the use of simple approximations to study dynamic face perception may not be appropriate in many situations. Furthermore, the finding that humans are very sensitive to natural facial motion dynamics raises the question of which cues humans extract from this detailed representation of facial motion.

Previous results suggested that the human face perception system may extract identity information from the representation of facial motion. However, the exact role of facial motion as cue for identity is still unclear (O'Toole et al., 2002). Our facial animation stimuli allow us to precisely investigate which facial movements contain identity information and how efficiently the face perception system extracts this information. We hypothesized that perception of identity information from facial motion might vary with the type of facial movement. In line with our hypothesis, in Chapter 3, we found that the amount of identity information and humans' sensitivity to this information vary with the type of facial movement. In contrast to previous models (Haxby et al., 2000), our results thus indicate a stronger interaction between the processing of facial motion and identity. A direct practical implication of these results is that functional magnetic resonance studies should be able to tease apart the brain structures that are specialized for processing identity information in facial movements. However, if facial movements contain information about the expression and the identity of a face, how does the human brain disentangle the representation of these two features?

Given the high sensitivity to natural facial motion and the strong interaction between facial motion and identity processing, we hypothesized that there is a neural mechanism which selectively extracts identity and expression information from dynamic faces depending on what information is needed. In Chapter 4, we found that when attending to the expression versus the identity of dynamic faces, representations of exemplars within these features were enhanced with attention. Moreover, identity was represented in cortical areas even when expression was attended. These results can be linked with the findings reported in Chapter 3: Identity information may be processed more automatically than expression information, thus allowing the face perception system to extract identity information even when expression is attended. Furthermore, our results indicate that identity information is transferred from areas processing invariant aspects of faces to areas processing changeable aspects via OFA, and that both sources of information may be integrated in area STS.

1.6 Conclusion

Humans effortlessly extract and process relevant cues from the rich source of information provided by dynamic faces. The results of the current thesis contribute to our understanding of the behavioral and neural mechanisms which underlie the processing of dynamic faces.

First, our results demonstrate how exquisitely sensitive the human perceptual system is to degradations of the spatio-temporal properties of natural facial motion. Furthermore, our facial animation stimuli allowed a quantitative explanation of observers' perceptual choices revealing the importance of meaningful spatio-temporal cues in the processing of facial motion. Second, our results reveal that the amount of identity information in facial motion varies with the type of facial movement. More specifically, the rather stereotypical emotional facial movements contain less identity information than facial movements performed in unconstrained contexts. From a theoretical viewpoint, this allows to bridge the gap between the fast interpretation of emotional facial expressions and the identity-specific processing of conversational and speech-related facial movements. Lastly, our results show an enhanced representation of high-level facial features with attention across multiple stages of the visual face processing system. Thus, they suggest that the representation of facial features in cortical areas change dynamically, and that attention acts as a mechanism to boost the representations of these high-level facial features. Moreover, our results indicate that identity information may be processed more automatically than expression information, thus allowing us to extract identity information even when the facial expression is attended.

These conclusions further validate attempts to capture and render semantically meaningful information in facial motion. Such methods are essential for a systematic, quantitative analysis of the great amount of information that can be conveyed by facial motion and have important implications for theories and models of facial motion perception.

1.7 References

Allison, T., Ginter, H., McCarthy, G., Nobre, A. C., Puce, A., Luby, M., & Spencer, D. D. (1994). Face recognition in human extrastriate cortex. Journal of Neurophysiology, 71, 821–821.

Allison, T., Puce, A., & McCarthy, G. (2000). Social perception from visual cues: role of the STS region. Trends in Cognitive Sciences, 4(7), 267–278.

Ambadar, Z., Schooler, J. W., & Cohn, J. F. (2005). Deciphering the enigmatic face the importance of facial dynamics in interpreting subtle facial expressions. Psychological Science, 16(5), 403–410.

Atkinson, A. P., Vuong, Q. C., & Smithson, H. E. (2012). Modulation of the face- and body-selective visual regions by the motion and emotion of point-light face and body stimuli. NeuroImage, 59(2), 1700–1712. doi:10.1016/j.neuroimage.2011.08.073

Bassili, J. N. (1978). Facial motion in the perception of faces and of emotional expression. Journal of Experimental Psychology: Human Perception and Performance, 4(3), 373.

Bernstein, L. E., Tucker, P. E., & Demorest, M. E. (2000). Speech perception without hearing. Perception & Psychophysics, 62(2), 233–252.

Berry, D. S. (1991). Child and Adult Sensitivity to Gender Information in Patterns of Facial Motion. Ecological Psychology, 3(4), 349–366. doi:10.1207/s15326969eco0304_3

Bruce, V., & Young, A. (1986). Understanding face recognition. British Journal of Psychology, 77(3), 305–327.

Calder, A. J., & Young, A. W. (2005). Understanding the recognition of facial identity and facial expression. Nature Reviews Neuroscience, 6(8), 641–651. doi:10.1038/nrn1724

Cohn, J. F., Schmidt, K., Gross, R., & Ekman, P. (2002). Individual differences in facial expression: Stability over time, relation to self-reported emotion, and ability to inform person identification, 491.

Cook, R., Matei, M., & Johnston, A. (2011). Exploring expression space: Adaptation to orthogonal and anti-expressions. Journal of Vision, 11(4), 2–2. doi:10.1167/11.4.2

Cunningham, D. W., & Wallraven, C. (2009). Dynamic information for the recognition of conversational expressions. Journal of Vision, 9(13), 7–7. doi:10.1167/9.13.7

Curio, C., Breidt, M., Kleiner, M., Vuong, Q. C., Giese, M. A., & Bülthoff, H. H. (2006). Semantic 3d motion retargeting for facial animation, 77–84.

Ekman, P., Friesen, W. V., & Hager, J. C. (2002). The Facial Action Coding System. Salt Lake City, UT: A Human Face.

Ekman, P., & Friesen, W. V. (1978). Facial Action Coding System: A technique for the measurement of facial movement. Palo Alto, CA: Consulting Psychologists Press.

Fairhall, S. L., & Ishai, A. (2007). Effective Connectivity within the Distributed Cortical Network for Face Perception. Cerebral Cortex, 17(10), 2400–2406. doi:10.1093/cercor/bhl148

Foley, E., Rippon, G., Thai, N. J., Longe, O., & Senior, C. (2012). Dynamic facial expressions evoke distinct activation in the face perception network: a connectivity analysis study. Journal of Cognitive Neuroscience, 24(2), 507–520.

Fox, C. J., Iaria, G., & Barton, J. J. S. (2009). Defining the face processing network: Optimization of the functional localizer in fMRI. Human Brain Mapping, 30(5), 1637–1651. doi:10.1002/hbm.20630

Furey, M. L., Tanskanen, T., Beauchamp, M. S., Avikainen, S., Uutela, K., Hari, R., & Haxby, J. V. (2006). Dissociation of face-selective cortical responses by attention. Proceedings of the National Academy of Sciences, 103(4), 1065–1070.

Furl, N., Henson, R. N., Friston, K. J., & Calder, A. J. (2014). Network Interactions Explain Sensitivity to Dynamic Faces in the Superior Temporal Sulcus. Cerebral Cortex. doi:10.1093/cercor/bhu083

Furl, N., van Rijsbergen, N. J., Kiebel, S. J., Friston, K. J., Treves, A., & Dolan, R. J. (2010). Modulation of Perception and Brain Activity by Predictable Trajectories of Facial Expressions. Cerebral Cortex, 20(3), 694–703. doi:10.1093/cercor/bhp140

Gauthier, I., & Logothetis, N. K. (2000). Is face recognition not so unique after all? Cognitive Neuropsychology, 17(1-3), 125–142.

Haxby, J. V., Hoffman, E. A., & Gobbini, M. I. (2000). The distributed human neural system for face perception. Trends in Cognitive Sciences, 4(6), 223–233.

Hill, H., & Johnston, A. (2001). Categorizing sex and identity from the biological motion of faces. Current Biology, 11(11), 880–885.

Hoffman, E. A., & Haxby, J. V. (2000). Distinct representations of eye gaze and identity in the distributed human neural system for face perception. Nature Neuroscience, 3(1), 80–84.

Jack, R. E., Garrod, O. G., Yu, H., Caldara, R., & Schyns, P. G. (2012). Facial expressions of emotion are not culturally universal. Proceedings of the National Academy of Sciences, 109(19), 7241–7244. doi:10.1073/pnas.1200155109/-/DCSupplemental/sm01.avi

Kamachi, M., Bruce, V., Mukaida, S., Gyoba, J., Yoshikawa, S., & Akamatsu, S. (2001). Dynamic properties influence the perception of facial expressions. Perception, 30(7), 875–887. doi:10.1068/p3131

Kanwisher, N., McDermott, J., & Chun, M. M. (1997). The fusiform face area: a module in human extrastriate cortex specialized for face perception. The Journal of Neuroscience, 17(11), 4302–4311.

Kaulard, K., Cunningham, D. W., Bülthoff, H. H., & Wallraven, C. (2012). The MPI Facial Expression Database — A Validated Database of Emotional and Conversational Facial Expressions. PLoS ONE, 7(3), e32321. doi:10.1371/journal.pone.0032321.s002

Knappmeyer, B., Thornton, I. M., & Bülthoff, H. H. (2003). The use of facial motion and facial form during the processing of identity. Vision Research, 43(18), 1921–1936. doi:10.1016/S0042-6989(03)00236-0

Ku, J., Jang, H. J., Kim, K. U., Kim, J. H., Park, S. H., Lee, J. H., et al. (2005). Experimental results of affective valence and arousal to avatar's facial expressions. CyberPsychology & Behavior, 8(5), 493–503.

LaBar, K. S., Crupain, M. J., Voyvodic, J. T., & McCarthy, G. (2003). Dynamic perception of facial affect and identity in the human brain. Cerebral Cortex, 13(10), 1023–1033.

Lander, K., & Bruce, V. (2003). The role of motion in learning new faces. Visual Cognition, 10(8), 897–912.

Lander, K., & Chuang, L. (2005). Why are moving faces easier to recognize? Visual Cognition, 12(3), 429–442. doi:10.1080/13506280444000382

Lander, K., Chuang, L., & Wickham, L. (2006). Recognizing face identity from natural and morphed smiles. The Quarterly Journal of Experimental Psychology, 59(05), 801–808. doi:10.1080/17470210600576136

Large, M.-E., Cavina-Pratesi, C., Vilis, T., & Culham, J. C. (2008). The neural correlates of change detection in the face perception network. Neuropsychologia, 46(8), 2169–2176. doi:10.1016/j.neuropsychologia.2008.02.027

Narumoto, J., Okada, T., Sadato, N., Fukui, K., & Yonekura, Y. (2001). Attention to emotion modulates fMRI activity in human right superior temporal sulcus. Cognitive Brain Research, 12(2), 225–231.

Nestor, A., Plaut, D. C., & Behrmann, M. (2011). Unraveling the distributed neural code of facial identity through spatiotemporal pattern analysis. Proceedings of the National Academy of Sciences, 108(24), 9998–10003. doi:10.1073/pnas.1102433108/-/DCSupplemental/pnas.201102433SI.pdf

O'Craven, K. M., Downing, P. E., & Kanwisher, N. (1999). fMRI evidence for objects as the units of attentional selection. Nature, 401(6753), 584–587.

O'Toole, A. J., Roark, D. A., & Abdi, H. (2002). Recognizing moving faces: A psychological and neural synthesis. Trends in Cognitive Sciences, 6(6), 261–266.

Parry, F. M., Young, A. W., Shona, J., & Saul, M. (1991). Dissociable face processing impairments after brain injury. Journal of Clinical and ....

Pitcher, D., Walsh, V., & Duchaine, B. (2011). The role of the occipital face area in the cortical face perception network. Experimental Brain Research, 209(4), 481–493. doi:10.1007/s00221-011-2579-1

Pollick, F. E., Hill, H., Calder, A., & Paterson, H. (2003). Recognising facial expression from spatially and temporally modified movements. Perception, 32(7), 813–826. doi:10.1068/p3319

Roark, D. A., Barrett, S. E., Spence, M., Herve, & O'Toole, A. J. (2003). Memory for moving faces: Psychological and Neural Perspectives on the Role of Motion in Face Recognition. Behavioral and Cognitive Neuroscience Reviews, 2(1), 15–46.

Roesch, E. B., Tamarit, L., Reveret, L., Grandjean, D., Sander, D., & Scherer, K. R. (2010). FACSGen: A Tool to Synthesize Emotional Facial Expressions Through Systematic Manipulation of Facial Action Units. Journal of Nonverbal Behavior, 35(1), 1–16. doi:10.1007/s10919-010-0095-9

Rosenblum, L. D., Yakel, D. A., Baseer, N., Panchal, A., Nodarse, B. C., & Niehus, R. P. (2002). Visual speech information for face recognition. Perception & Psychophysics, 64(2), 220–229.

Rotshtein, P., Henson, R. N. A., Treves, A., Driver, J., & Dolan, R. J. (2004). Morphing Marilyn into Maggie dissociates physical and identity face representations in the brain. Nature Neuroscience, 8(1), 107–113. doi:10.1038/nn1370

Sarkheil, P., Goebel, R., Schneider, F., & Mathiak, K. (2013). Emotion unfolded by motion: a role for parietal lobe in decoding dynamic facial expressions. Social Cognitive and Affective Neuroscience, 8(8), 950–957. doi:10.1093/scan/nss092

Sato, W., & Yoshikawa, S. (2007). Enhanced Experience of Emotional Arousal in Response to Dynamic Facial Expressions. Journal of Nonverbal Behavior, 31(2), 119–135. doi:10.1007/s10919-007-0025-7

Schultz, J., & Pilz, K. S. (2009). Natural facial motion enhances cortical responses to faces. Experimental Brain Research, 194(3), 465–475. doi:10.1007/s00221-009-1721-9

Schultz, J., Brockhaus, M., Bülthoff, H. H., & Pilz, K. S. (2013). What the Human Brain Likes About Facial Motion. Cerebral Cortex, 23(5), 1167–1178. doi:10.1093/cercor/bhs106

Schweinberger, S. R., & Soukup, G. R. (1998). Asymmetric relationships among perceptions of facial identity, emotion, and facial speech. Journal of Experimental Psychology: Human Perception and

Performance, 24(6), 1748.

Schweinberger, S. R., Burton, A. M., & Kelly, S. W. (1999). Asymmetric dependencies in perceiving identity and emotion: Experiments with morphed faces. Perception & Psychophysics, 61(6), 1102–1115.

Sergent, J., Ohta, S., & MacDonald, B. (1992). Functional neuroanatomy of face and object processing. A positron emission tomography study. Brain, 115(1), 15–36.

Sergent, J., Ohta, S., MacDonald, B., & Zuck, E. (1994). Segregated processing of facial identity and emotion in the human brain: A pet study. Visual Cognition, 1(2), 349–369. doi:10.1080/13506289408402305

Walder, C., Breidt, M., Bülthoff, H., Schölkopf, B., & Curio, C. (2009). Markerless 3d face tracking, 41–50.

Winston, J. S., Henson, R. N. A., Fine-Goulden, M. R., & Dolan, R. J. (2004). fMRI-Adaptation Reveals Dissociable Neural Representations of Identity and Expression in Face Perception. Journal of Neurophysiology, 92(3), 1830–1839. doi:10.1152/jn.00155.2004

Wojciulik, E., Kanwisher, N., & Driver, J. (1998). Covert visual attention modulates face-specific activity in the human fusiform gyrus: fMRI study. Journal of Neurophysiology, 79(3), 1574–1578.

Xu, X., & Biederman, I. (2010). Loci of the release from fMRI adaptation for changes in facial expression, identity, and viewpoint. Journal of Vision, 10(14), 36–36. doi:10.1167/10.14.36

Yu, H., Garrod, O. G. B., & Schyns, P. G. (2012). Computers & Graphics. Computers and Graphics, 36(3), 152–162. doi:10.1016/j.cag.2011.12.002

1.8 Declaration of Contribution

This thesis comprises of three manuscripts that are either accepted or prepared for publication. Details about these manuscripts are presented in the following.

The ideas for the studies, their experimental design and implementation were developed by the candidate. The data collection and analysis was performed by the candidate. The co-authors supervised the work of the candidate and assisted in the revision of the manuscripts.

1. Dobs, K., Bülthoff, I., Breidt, M., Vuong, Q. C., Curio, C., & Schultz, J. (2014). Quantifying human sensitivity to spatio-temporal information in dynamic faces. *Vision Research*, *100*, 78-87: Design, stimulus generation, experimental work and analysis of the study have predominantly been developed and finalized by the candidate. The co-authors' role was that of supervision in giving advice, offering knowledge and criticism, and revising the manuscript.

2. Dobs, K., Bülthoff, I., & Schultz, J. (2014). Identity information in facial motion varies with the type of facial movement. (prepared for submission): Design, stimulus generation, experimental work and analysis of the study have predominantly been developed and finalized by the candidate. The co-authors' role was that of supervision in giving advice, offering knowledge and criticism, and revising the manuscript.

3. Dobs, K., Schultz, J. W., Bülthoff, I., & Gardner, J. L. (2014). Attention to dynamic faces enhances the neural representation of expression and identity in the human face processing system. (prepared for submission): Design, stimulus generation, experimental work and analysis of the study have predominantly been developed and finalized by the candidate. The co-authors' role was that of supervision in giving advice, offering knowledge and criticism, and revising the manuscript.

Parts of this work was also presented at the following conferences:

1. Dobs, K., Bülthoff, I., & Schultz, J. (2014, March). *Neural and behavioural correlates of facial motion processing.* Paper presented at The Rank Prize Funds: Symposium on the Perception of Faces, Grasmere, UK.

2. Dobs, K., Schultz, J., Bülthoff, I., & Gardner, J.L. (2013, November). *Attending to expression or identity of dynamic faces engages different cortical areas.* Paper

presented at the 43rd Annual Meeting of the Society for Neuroscience: Neuroscience 2013, San Diego, CA, USA.

3. Dobs, K., Bülthoff, I., Breidt, M., Vuong, Q.C., Curio, C., & Schultz, J.W. (2013, August). Quantifying human sensitivity to spatio-temporal information in dynamic faces. Paper presented at the 36th European Conference on Visual Perception: ECVP 2013, Bremen, Germany, *Perception, 42*(ECVP Abstract Supplement), 197.

4. Dobs, K., Bülthoff, I., Curio, C., & Schultz, J. (2012, August). Investigating factors influencing the perception of identity from facial motion. Paper presented at the 12th Annual Meeting of the Vision Sciences Society: VSS 2012), Naples, FL, USA, *Journal of Vision, 12*(9), 35.

5. Dobs, K., Kleiner, M., Bülthoff, I., Schultz, J., & Curio, C. (2011, September). Investigating idiosyncratic facial dynamics with motion retargeting, Paper presented at the 34th European Conference on Visual Perception: ECVP 2011, Toulouse, France, *Perception, 40*(ECVP Abstract Supplement), 115.

2 Quantifying human sensitivity to spatio-temporal information in dynamic faces

This chapter has been reproduced from an article published in Vision Research: Dobs, K., Bülthoff, I., Breidt, M., Vuong, Q. C., Curio, C., & Schultz, J. (2014). Quantifying human sensitivity to spatio-temporal information in dynamic faces. *Vision Research, 100*, 78-87.

2.1 Abstract

A great deal of perceptual and social information is conveyed by facial motion. Here, we investigated observers' sensitivity to the complex spatio-temporal information in facial expressions and what cues they use to judge the similarity of these movements. We motion-captured four facial expressions and decomposed them into time courses of semantically meaningful local facial actions (e.g., eyebrow raise). We then generated approximations of the time courses which differed in the amount of information about the natural facial motion they contained, and used these and the original time courses to animate an avatar head. Observers chose which of two animations based on approximations was more similar to the animation based on the original time course. We found that observers preferred animations containing more information about the natural facial motion dynamics. To explain observers' similarity judgments, we developed and used several measures of objective stimulus similarity. The time course of facial actions (e.g., onset and peak of eyebrow raise) explained observers' behavioral choices better than image-based measures (e.g., optic flow). Our results thus revealed observers' sensitivity to changes of natural facial dynamics. Importantly, our method allows a quantitative explanation of the perceived similarity of dynamic facial expressions, which suggests that sparse but meaningful spatio-temporal cues are used to process facial motion.

2.2 Introduction

Most of the faces we encounter and interact with everyday move. Dynamic faces are highly ecological stimuli from which we can extract various cues such as the affective states of others (e.g., Ambadar, Schooler, & Cohn, 2005; Cunningham & Wallraven, 2009; Kaulard, Cunningham, Bülthoff, & Wallraven, 2012; Krumhuber, Kappas, & Manstead, 2013), the intensity of emotions (e.g., Jack, Garrod, Yu, Caldara, & Schyns, 2012;

23

Kamachi et al., 2001) or speech movements (e.g., Bernstein, Demorest, & Tucker, 2000; Rosenblum et al., 2002). Given the social relevance of facial motion, it is of great interest to study which face motion cues are used by observers during perceptual tasks. However, dynamic face information is complex, which makes it difficult to isolate and quantify meaningful cues. Such quantification would for example allow testing human sensitivity to various aspects of this spatio-temporal information (e.g., onset or acceleration of movements) using dynamic face stimuli with controlled information content. Here we first measured the perceived similarity of computer generated facial expressions. This similarity was then correlated with different cues in the animations to test observers' sensitivity to natural facial movements and explore the cues they used for face perception.

One common method to quantify the spatio-temporal information in complex facial movements is to use a coding scheme for facial expressions called Facial Action Coding System (FACS; Ekman, Friesen, & Hager, 2002; Ekman & Friesen, 1978). This system defines a number of discrete face movements - termed Action Units - as an intuitive and accurate description of the basic constituents of facial expressions (e.g., eyebrow raising). Each Action Unit can be represented as a time course which captures the magnitude of activation of a "local" facial region (e.g., eyebrow) over time. This magnitude can vary from no activation to some maximum intensity. As exemplified in Figure 1 (red line), the eyebrow can naturally rise and lower from a resting, neutral position over time as an actor makes a facial expression. These time courses thus capture spatio-temporal properties of local facial movements (e.g., onset, acceleration of eyebrow raising). Curio and colleagues developed a novel 3D facial animation approach inspired by FACS to decompose motion-capture data recorded from actors into time courses of local facial movements termed facial actions (Curio et al, 2006). Like Action Units of the FACS system, facial actions are semantically meaningful. In their study, Curio and colleagues showed that using a set of local facial actions to approximate the facial motion led to more natural animations than using a global approximation in which the whole face is deformed at the same time.

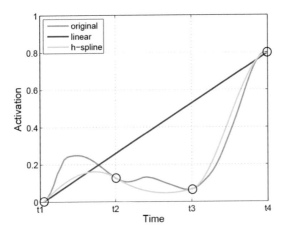

Figure 1. Exemplary time course of activation for one local facial action. The "original" time course derived from facial motion tracking is shown in red. The simplest kind of approximation is a "linear interpolation" from t1 to t4 (outer left and outer right black circles) of the original time course, and is shown in blue. A more sophisticated approximation method is to use a Hermite spline interpolation ("h-spline"), based on four control points (t1, t2, t3 and t4, black circles), which is shown in green.

Recently, a series of studies have used synthesized time courses for FACS Action Units to generate animations of facial expressions in the absence of actor data (e.g., Jack et al., 2012; Roesch et al., 2011; Yu et al., 2012). Without real-data recorded from a performing actor, the particular shape of an Action Unit's time course is arbitrary, and various methods can be used to generate it. In its simplest form, an Action Unit's activation can increase linearly over time from no activation to some level of activation (see blue line in Figure 1). When applying this linear interpolation to all Action Units of a facial expression, the resulting stimulus is very similar to an image sequence made by gradually morphing between two images (e.g., neutral and peak of the facial expression). Given the simplicity and ease of control, such techniques have been used in many studies investigating facial motion perception (e.g., Furl et al., 2010; Ku et al., 2005; LaBar, Crupain, Voyvodic, & McCarthy, 2003; Sarkheil et al., 2012; Sato & Yoshikawa, 2007). More recent studies have combined spline interpolation (see green line in Figure 1) with advanced reverse-correlation methods and found that observers used fine-grained spatio-temporal cues to categorize facial expressions (e.g., Jack et al., 2012; Yu et al., 2012). In line with these findings, other studies showed that advanced spatio-temporal interpolations are perceived as more natural than linear or global interpolations of facial motion (e.g., Cosker, Krumhuber, & Hilton, 2010; Curio et al., 2006). However, how sensitive humans are to spatio-temporal cues in facial motion has not been investigated quantitatively so far.

In the current study, we investigated observers' sensitivity to changes in facial motion, and studied what cues observers extract and interpret when making judgments about facial motion. Identifying these cues would provide clues about the importance of different aspects of facial motion for perception, also in comparison to static faces, and thus have implications for theories of mental representations of facial motion. Given the importance of motion for facial expressions, we focused on this aspect of face perception but it should be noted that identity and expressions may be processed by different pathways in the brain (Bruce & Young, 1986; Haxby, Hoffman, & Gobbini, 2002; but see also Calder & Young, 2005). With static faces, one widely used approach to determine cues important for face perception is to correlate objective measures of similarity (e.g., Gabor jets, principal components) with perceived similarities between facial expressions (e.g., Lyons et al., 1998; Susskind et al., 2007) and facial identities (e.g., Rhodes, 1988; Steyvers & Busey, 2000; Yue et al., 2012). Here we adopted a similar approach for dynamic facial expressions to assess whether objective measures of facial motion similarity could explain the perceived similarity of facial motion. As discussed below, the different measures captured both low-level and high-level cues in our dynamic faces. We used the system developed by Curio and colleagues (2006) to generate high quality animations based on natural facial motion, which we will refer to as "original animations". We then created additional animations based on different approximations of the facial action time courses obtained from the actors' motion, which we will call "approximations". To this end, we chose interpolation techniques such that the approximations systematically varied in the amount of information they contained about the natural motion dynamics. Observers judged which of two approximations was more similar to the original animation. If observers were sensitive to differences between the approximations, they would consistently judge one animation of the pair to be more similar to the original. We captured facial expressions with different dynamics (e.g., including speech movements) to investigate whether the goodness of an approximation varied with the type of facial expression. The pattern of choices served as a measure of the perceived similarity between approximations and the original animation, and allowed us to directly compare perceived similarities between stimuli with objective measures of similarity. Here, we calculated these objective similarity measures based on three kinds of information: (1) time courses of facial action activation, (2) optic flow, and (3) Gabor-jet filters. Importantly, facial action time courses capture semantically meaningful high-level changes to a sparse set of local facial regions (e.g., eyebrow) whereas optic flow and Gabor-jets capture detailed low-level image changes (e.g., movement direction of one pixel). To anticipate our results: We found that high-level cues about spatio-temporal characteristics of facial motion best explained observers' choice pattern.

2.3 Material and methods

Participants

Fourteen participants (6 female; mean age: 28.6 ± 5.2 years) were recruited from the subject database of the Max Planck Institute for Biological Cybernetics, Tübingen, Germany. They were naive to the purpose of the experiment and had normal or corrected-to-normal vision. All participants provided informed written consent prior to the experiment and filled out a post-questionnaire after the experiment was finished. The study was conducted in accordance to the Declaration of Helsinki.

Stimuli

To create highly controllable and accurate animations of facial expressions, we used a system that decomposes recorded motion data into time courses of facial actions (e.g., eyebrow raising) which are used to animate a 3D head model with corresponding facial actions (Curio et al., 2006). This facial animation procedure is schematically shown in Figure 2 and is explained in detail in Appendix A.

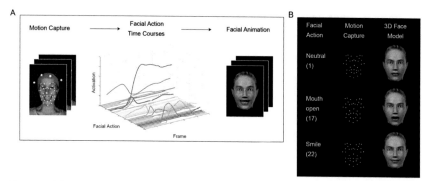

Figure 2. (A) Schematic overview of the facial animation procedure, shown for the facial expression happiness. In the first step, motion capture data from a set of facial actions and the facial expression happiness is recorded from the actor (left). In the second step, the facial animation system decomposes the motion capture data of the facial expression into time courses of facial action activation (middle). In the last step, the time courses of facial action activation are used to animate a semantically matched 3D face model (right). (B) Three example facial actions "Neutral" (facial action 1), "Mouth open" (facial action 17) and "Smile" (facial action 22). The recorded facial marker positions for the facial actions (middle), and the semantically matched 3D facial action shapes created for the 3D face model (right).

Constructing approximations of natural facial expressions

We created approximations of the original time courses for each facial action obtained from the motion decomposition (see Appendix A for details). We did not attempt to find the optimal technique to approximate natural facial motion, but focused on different approximation techniques (linear and spline interpolations) previously used to investigate perception of facial motion (e.g., Jack et al., 2012; Sarkheil et al., 2012). We selected different time points at fixed intervals of the original time courses as control points to create our approximations. The start and the end of the time course were always included as control points but the number of points in between was varied to create approximations that preserved different aspects of the original time course. We selected a subset of four approximation techniques to span a range of possible techniques. Many more techniques could have been used to reveal a more fine-grained pattern of results; however, restrictions imposed by the experimental design (mainly the total number of trials) meant that this would have gone beyond the scope of the present study.

Figure 3 illustrates the four approximation techniques we used, with the facial action "mouth open" from the facial expression "fear" serving as example. The red line represents the time course from the motion decomposition (*orig*, Figure 3A and 3B). For the linear approximation *lin1* (magenta, Figure 3A), three equidistant control points were chosen from the original time course (frame 1, 50 and 100, black circles) and used to linearly interpolate the original time course. The second approximation *lin2* (blue, Figure 3B) is another linear interpolation of the original time course based on four equidistant control points (frame 1, 33, 67 and 100, black circles). Lin2 contains more information about the original time courses than lin1, and the animation made on its basis should thus be perceived as more similar to the animation based on the original time course. Linear interpolations may contain sharp changes in the time courses at the position of the control points (see frame 67 of lin2, black circle in Figure 3B). The visual system may be sensitive to these changes. Thus, for another set of approximations, we created spline interpolations of the original time courses, which are very smooth at the control points and should thus appear more similar to the original motion than lin1 and lin2. For the first spline approximation *spl1* (green in Figure 3A) we used a cubic spline interpolation based on the same three control points as lin1 (frame 1, 50 and 100, black circles). While this approximation is smoother than the linear approximations, splines tend to exceed (overshoot) the interpolated time course at extremes, resulting in a large difference from the original time course. We reduced this in the next approximation by using cubic Hermite splines *hspl* (yellow, Figure 3B), in which the spline interpolation not only goes through the same four control points as lin2 (frame 1, 33, 67 and 100, black circles) but also preserves the slope of the time course at the given control points. This approximation contains the most information about the original time courses of facial actions.

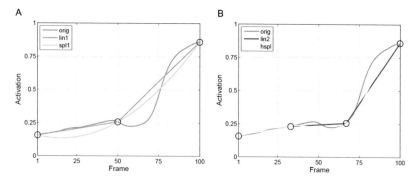

Figure 3. Time course of activation for the facial action "Mouth open" during the facial expression "fear" directly resulting from the motion analysis (orig, shown in red) and interpolated using four approximation types. (A) Approximations lin1 (magenta) and spl1 (green) based on three control points (frame 1, 50 and 100, black circles). (B) Approximations lin2 (blue) and hspl (yellow) based on four control points (frame 1, 33, 67 and 100, black circles).

Animation stimuli

For each facial expression, we sub-sampled the number of frames by a factor of three to 34 frames to ensure fluid video display during the experiments (Note: this down-sampling did not affect the smoothness or other characteristics of the time courses and was thus not perceptible in the final stimuli). We then loaded the original and approximated time courses of facial action activation into 3ds Max to produce 20 Quicktime animation movies with a resolution of 480 x 640 pixels, a duration of about 1 s (34 frames at 30Hz), and scene and rendering settings optimized for facial animations.

To assess whether our stimuli could be correctly recognized, we performed a preliminary experiment with a different set of participants (N=10). In a 4 alternative-forced-choice task, participants were able to correctly identify the four expressions from the animations based on the original time courses (chance = 25%). Recognition was perfect for happiness (mean and standard error of the mean: 100% ± 0%) and good for anger and surprise (80% ± 13% for both). Performance for the expression fear was lower but still clearly above chance level (60% ± 16%).

Videos that matched the animations frame-by-frame were recorded by the scene camera during the motion capture, and after scaling to match the visual angle subtended by the size of the face in the animations (approximately 8° x 13°), they were saved at the same frame rate as the animations. We used these videos as stimuli in a

30

second preliminary experiment which tested whether the original animation was perceptually the most similar to the corresponding expression video. The participants of our main study (N = 14, see section 2.3) performed a delayed match-to-sample task using the video as sample and the animations as comparison stimuli. When paired with any approximation, the original animation was chosen in more than 50% for all expressions (anger: 89%, $t(13) = 18.97, p < 0.0001$; fear: 69%, $t(13) = 9.33, p < 0.0001$; happiness: 71%, $t(13) = 5.37, p < 0.001$; surprise: 72%, $t(13) = 7.11, p < 0.0001$). Thus, the original animations were perceived to be most similar to videos of the expressions.

Design and procedure

Perceptual sensitivity to the different approximations was tested in a delayed match-to-sample task: After watching the original animation driven by one of the four facial expressions (sample), observers were asked to indicate which of the two approximations (matching stimuli A and B) was most similar to the original animation. The six possible combinations of the four approximations were repeated ten times (60 trials) for each of the four facial expressions, for a total of 240 trials. Trials were run in random order and the presentation on the left or the right side of the screen was counter-balanced for each animation within a specific pair.

Figure 4 depicts the trial procedure in the experiment. All trials began with a white fixation cross on a black background shown for 0.5 s at the center of the screen, followed by the original animation. After the animation, a black screen appeared for 0.5 s, followed by two matching animations presented side-by-side, 6.7° to the left and right of fixation. As the difference between animations was subtle, we decided to present the animations simultaneously to allow for detailed, continuous assessment of the facial motions without influence of memory load. The same presentation procedure had already been successfully used in the study by Curio et al. (2006). Observers could indicate their readiness to respond by pressing any key on a standard computer keyboard during the trial. The sequence of animation, black screen and two animations was repeated until a key was pressed or three presentations were reached. Each sequence was repeated 1.45 times per trial on average across observers with a standard deviation of 0.31. Then a response screen showing the question "Which of the two animations was most similar to the original?" appeared. Observers pressed the left or right cursor arrow key to choose the corresponding animation. The response screen remained until observers responded. No feedback was provided.

Observers could take up to seven self-timed breaks, one every 30 trials. The experiment lasted approximately 60-70 minutes and was programmed using PsychToolbox 3 for Matlab (http://www.psychtoolbox.org) (Kleiner, 2010). Observers were seated approximately 68 cm from a Dell 2407WFP monitor (24 inch screen diagonal size, 1920 x 1200 pixel resolution; 60Hz refresh rate).

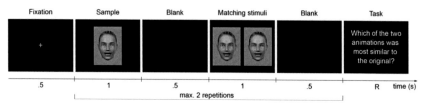

Figure 4. The trial procedure of the experiment.

Calculating objective similarity measures

One aim of this experiment was to determine the extent to which observers' choice behavior correlated with objective measures of similarity between the animations. Each stimulus consists of a sequence of images (34 frames). Given how each animation was generated, an animation stimulus can also be conceived as a set of time courses (with each time course representing the activation of a facial action over time). Various cues can thus be extracted from either the image sequences or the time courses and used to measure the similarity between two animations.

Similarity based on facial action activation

First, we calculated the similarity of animations based on the time courses of facial action activation. Each frame of the original animation and the approximations can be described in terms of the activation of facial actions used to construct this frame. As those values cannot be retrieved in a straightforward way using image analysis, we consider these facial action activations to be high-level cues. To calculate the similarity between two animations, we carried out the following steps. First, we interpreted each frame of an animation as coordinates in an n-dimensional facial action space, where n represents the number of facial actions used to generate a frame of the stimulus. For a single frame, we computed the distance between two animations in this space as the Euclidean distance between the facial action activations. We then summed the distances across all frames. This procedure was implemented in the following equation, for two animations a and b:

$$d_{FA}(a, b) = \sum_{i=1}^{m} \sqrt{\sum_{j=1}^{n} (a_{i,j} - b_{i,j})^2} \quad , \tag{1}$$

where $m = 34$ is the total number of frames per animation, $n = 30$ is the number of facial actions and $a_{i,j}$ represents the activation level of facial action j at time i. Note that the same equation can be applied to calculate the similarity between two animations based on a subset of facial actions, or even based on a single facial action (e.g., for facial action "eyebrows raised" with $n = 1$).

Similarity based on optic flow.

Second, we calculated the similarity between two animations based on optic flow. In the context of an image sequence, optic flow is defined as the spatial displacement of pixels from one image of the animation to the next image (Horn & Schunck, 1981). We used 3ds Max to directly output the pixel motion of our animations (called "velocity render element" in the software). The motion output of one time frame consists of q 3-dimensional vectors of pixel space motion (x-, y- and z-motion), where q represents the number of pixels in the animation. For simplicity, we ignored motion in the z-axis (depth) as the stimuli rendered from our animations were 2-dimensional. We calculated the distance in pixel motion between two animations a and b as follows:

$$d_{OF}(a, b) = \sum_{i=1}^{m-1} \sum_{p=1}^{q} \sqrt{\sum_{c=1}^{2} (a_{i,p,c} - b_{j,p,c})^2} \quad , \tag{2}$$

where c represents the motion direction (in horizontal and vertical dimensions), $q = 480 \times 640$ is the number of pixels p per frame, summed over m (the total number of frames per animation) $-1 = 33$ consecutive pairs of frames. (Note that the sum is over m-1 frames as the motion vectors represent pixel motion from two consecutive frames, so there is no motion information about the first frame of the animation.)

33

Gabor similarity

As a third similarity measure, we computed the Gabor similarity between two animations. Gabor similarity is a biologically-inspired physical similarity measure that emulates the responses of simple and complex cells (see Lades et al., 1993). In early visual cortex (V1), both simple and complex cells are organized into hypercolumns that respond to different spatial frequencies at different orientations. Importantly, this similarity measure is highly correlated with the perceived similarity of the identity of static faces (e.g., Yue et al., 2012) and has been successfully applied as similarity measure for facial expressions (Xu & Biederman, 2010). We computed the Gabor similarity between two animations as follows. First, we took all corresponding frames from each animation and converted them into grayscale images (256 levels). Second, we placed a Gabor jet at the intersections of a uniform grid (11 x 14) covering the entire image. Each jet consisted of five spatial scales and eight equidistant orientations (i.e., 22.5° differences in angle; for details see Yue et al., 2012). Third, we convolved the image with each jet to get its response to an image. The responses from all the Gabor jets thus form a high-dimensional feature vector (5 scales x 8 orientations x (11 x 14) jets = 6160 features) for each frame. Lastly, the Gabor similarity between corresponding images was computed as the Euclidean distance between the two feature vectors, J_a and J_b, and summed across all corresponding pairs of frames in the two animations a and b:

$$d_{GS}(a,b) = \sum_{i=1}^{m} \sqrt{\sum_{j=1}^{n} \left(J_{a_{i,j}} - J_{b_{i,j}}\right)^2} \quad , \tag{3}$$

where m = 34 represents the number of frames and n is the number of features in each feature vector.

Calculating choice probabilities

In order to compare the objective similarity measures to observers' choice behavior, we computed choice probabilities based on the three objective similarity measures (Luce, 1959). Observers had to choose which of two approximations was most similar to the original animation. For each similarity measure, we used Luce's choice rule to calculate the probability of choosing one approximation over the other. The probability of choosing which of two approximations, a and b, is most similar to the original animation can be expressed as the conditional probability of selecting a (response r_a) given an original animation o:

$$P(r_a|o) = 1 - \frac{d(a|o)}{d(a|o) + d(b|o)} \quad ,$$

(4)

where $d(a,o)$ is the similarity between the approximation a and the original animation o in terms of facial action activation, optic flow or Gabor similarity, and $d(b,o)$ is the corresponding similarity between approximation b and the original o. Note that the choice probability is given as 1- fraction because the similarity is represented as distance, such that large distances indicate low similarity and small distances indicate high similarity. If two approximations are equally similar to the original animation o (i.e., $d(a,o) = d(b,o)$), the probability of choosing a is 0.5. If the approximation a is very similar to the original animation o (e.g., the distance $d(a,o) = 0.1$) and the approximation b is very dissimilar (e.g., the distance $d(b,o) = 0.9$), the probability of choosing a is very high (e.g., $P(r_a/o) = 0.9$).

Regression analyses

We investigated whether the calculated choice probabilities based on objective similarity measures could predict observers' choice behavior. After assessment of the normality of the data (quantile-quantile plot of data against a normal distribution), we ran three separate linear regression analyses to assess the contribution of each similarity measure to the behavioral choices. A Kolmogorov-Smirnov test on the residuals was not significant and thus confirmed the suitability of parametric analyses. Second, we investigated the best fitting model combining the three similarity measures to explain the behavioral choices. As facial action time courses are used to create the animation stimuli which image-based measures are based on, we expected the similarity measures to be correlated. In case of multicollinearity, the prediction accuracy of ordinary least squares regression can be reduced and the results are difficult to interpret (e.g., see Hoerl & Kennard, 1970). Compared to ordinary least squares regression, regularized regression obtains higher prediction accuracy (in particular if multicollinearity exists) and provides a simpler model by selecting the most informative predictors. Regularized regression methods include an additional regularization term in the cost function (e.g., an l_1-norm regularizer as in the "Lasso method"; see Tibshirani, 1996; or an l_2-norm as in "ridge regression"; see Hoerl & Kennard, 1970) for which a regularization parameter λ defines the degree to which coefficients are penalized. While ridge regression performs a shrinking of all coefficients, Lasso additionally selects variables by setting small coefficients to zero. Recently, a regularized regression method was proposed which combines Lasso and ridge regression (called "Elastic net"; see Zou & Hastie, 2005). Elastic net selects the most important predictors under consideration of multicollinearity (Zou & Hastie, 2005) where an additional parameter α ($0 < \alpha <= 1$) defines the weight of lasso ($\alpha = 1$) versus ridge regression ($\alpha = 0$). Here, we applied regularized regression to investigate which similarity measure could explain most of the variance in the behavioral choices.

2.4 Results

Observers' perceptual choices

Figure 5 shows which approximation the observers judged to be perceptually closest to the original animation in all possible pairs (Figure 5A) and separated for facial expressions (Figure 5B). The y-axis represents the mean proportion of trials in which observers chose a specific approximation and the x-axis represents the six possible approximation pairs. For trials in which approximation A was paired with approximation B, 0 indicates that B (bottom label on x-axis) was chosen on 100% of the trials, 1 indicates that A (top label of x-axis) was chosen on 100% of the trials, and 0.5 indicates that both approximations were chosen equally often.

As can be seen in Figure 5A, choice proportion was different from chance in all pairs (lin2 > lin1: 70%, $t(13) = 9.91$, $p < 0.0001$, $d = 2.65$; hspl > lin1: 76%, $t(13) = 9.96$, $p < 0.0001$, $d = 2.53$; lin2 > spl1: 69%, $t(13) = 9.46$, $p < 0.0001$, $d = 2.46$; lin2 > lin2: 66%, $t(13) = 9.26$, $p < 0.0001$, $d = 2.66$; hspl > spl1: 69%, $t(13) = 9.19$, $p < 0.0001$, $d = 2.48$) except for the pair lin1-spl1 (lin1 > spl1: 56%, $t(13) = 1.08$, $p > 0.1$, $d = 0.29$). This result suggests that observers were sensitive to differences between approximations because they consistently chose one approximation over another, with the exception of lin1 and spl1 (chosen equally often). The data further show that the four animations can be ranked in terms of observers' decreasing choice proportion: hspl > lin2 > lin1 = spl1.

36

A 6 approximation pairs x 4 expressions ANOVA revealed a main effect of approximation pair on choice proportions ($F(5,13)$ = 81.49; p < 0.0001, η^2 = 0.474). Choices also varied as a function of expression ($F(3,13)$ = 8.3; p < 0.001, η^2 = 0.026). Lastly, an interaction between the two factors ($F(15,195)$ = 14.93; p < 0.0001, η^2 = 0.192; see Figure 5B) revealed that observers' choices were not consistent across different facial expressions, suggesting that there was not one specific approximation that was perceived to be most similar to the original animation for all expressions.

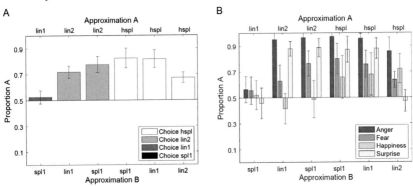

Figure 5. Behavioral results. Proportion of approximation A choices for each pair of two approximations A and B (A), and as a function of facial expression (B). Error bars indicate 95% confidence interval (CI) in all plots. A choice proportion of 0.5 indicates that both approximations were chosen equally often (50%), a proportion of 1 indicates that approximation A was always chosen in this pair. The approximations can be ranked in decreasing order of observers' choice proportion: hspl > lin2 > lin1 = spl1.

Explaining observers' perceptual choices

We investigated whether the calculated choice probabilities based on the three objective measures of similarity could explain the behavioral choice pattern. First, we assessed their separate contribution using linear regression. To this end, we calculated three separate linear regression analyses, in each of which only one measure was used as predictor and the choice behavior was the predicted measure. All predictors could significantly explain the variance of the behavioral choices. The choice probabilities based on facial action activation were highly predictive and explained 59% of the variance (r = 0.77, p < 0.0001), indicating that the semantically meaningful facial actions capture spatio-temporal properties which are used for judging similarity between facial expressions. The choice probabilities based on physical similarity measures also explained variance of the behavioral choices, with more variance explained by optic flow (r = 0.74, 54% variance explained, $p < 0.0001$) than Gabor similarity (r = 0.60, 36% variance explained, $p < 0.01$). This finding suggests that motion cues measured by optic flow are closer to cues used for perceiving motion similarity than cues extracted by the biologically motivated V1-based Gabor similarity.

As the animation stimuli were based on time courses of facial action activation, we expected the choice probabilities based on facial action activation to be correlated with choice probabilities based on the physical characteristics of the animations (optic flow and Gabor similarity measures). We found that choice probabilities based on facial action similarity measure significantly correlated with choice probabilities based on both Gabor similarity measure (r = 0.83, $p < 0.001$) and on optic flow-based similarity measure (r = 0.88; $p < 0.001$). These results suggest that, unsurprisingly, the time courses of facial action activation used to create the animations capture physical properties of the resulting animation well. However, compared to image-based measurements, facial action time courses reflect these physical properties in a semantically meaningful and sparse representation.

Selecting the best fitting model

We investigated which model based on the three objective measures of similarity could best explain the behavioral choice pattern. In this analysis, the 24 behavioral choice proportions (6 approximation pair types x 4 facial expressions) were the predicted measure and the 3 x 24 choice probabilities obtained from the three objective similarity measures were predictors. As the choice probabilities based on image cues were highly correlated with the choice probabilities based on facial action activation, we chose elastic net as regularized regression and variable selection method (Zou & Hastie, 2005). The results of the elastic net fitting using α = 0.5 (we chose α to equally weight between lasso and ridge regression) and 10-fold cross validation are shown in Figure 6. The standardized coefficients for each predictor (facial action activation in grey, optic flow in orange, Gabor similarity in light blue) are plotted as a function of λ. With increasing values of λ, elastic net retains optic flow and facial action activation as nonzero coefficients while the latter is set to zero last. Note that for λ = 0, the coefficients are equivalent to ordinary least squares regression. The dashed vertical lines represent λ with minimal mean prediction squared error (λ = 0.06, MSE = 0.03;

dashed black line) and the MSE plus one standard deviation (λ = 0.21; red dashed line) as calculated by cross-validation. The best fitting model with λ = 0.06 explained 61% of the variance in the behavioral choices (R = 0.78; $F(13)$ = 33.77; p < 0.0001). The fitted coefficients for this model were Beta = 0.88 for facial action activation, Beta = 0.46 for optic flow and Beta = 0 for Gabor similarity. The results suggest that the best model (i.e., the highest prediction accuracy with minimal predictors) to predict the behavioral choices is based on both facial action activation and optic flow.

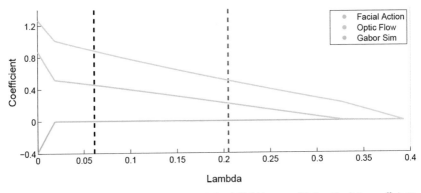

Figure 6. The result of elastic net fitting using α = 0.5 and 10-fold cross validation. Predictor coefficients (y-axis; facial action activation in grey, optic flow in orange, Gabor similarity in light blue) are plotted as a function of the regularization parameter λ (x-axis). The black dashed vertical line represents the λ value with minimal mean squared error (MSE). The λ value with minimal MSE plus one standard deviation is shown by the red dashed line.

2.5 Discussion

When we see a person smile, we see how local face parts such as the mouth and the eyebrows move naturally over time. In this study, we show that observers are highly sensitive to deviations from the natural motions of face parts. Using different approximations of these natural motions, we found that observers could not only discriminate between the different approximations, but that they were sensitive to the amount of information about the natural motion given by those approximations. The more information about the natural original motion (e.g., control points along the natural motion curve) was used to create an approximation, the more similar to the original animation it appeared. These results are consistent with previous findings (e.g.,

Cosker et al., 2010; Curio et al., 2006; Furl et al., 2010; Pollick, Hill, Calder, & Paterson, 2003; Wallraven, Breidt, Cunningham, & Bülthoff, 2008) and emphasize the importance of the quality of the approximation of facial motion in order to study perception of dynamic faces. Our results extend this previous work by showing a quantitative relationship between, on the one hand, the amount of information about natural motion contained in an approximation, and on the other hand, the perceived similarity between an approximation and a reproduction of natural motion.

It is important to notice that the perceived similarity of an approximation to the original animation varied with the type of facial expressions shown in our study. Facial movements may have different complexities in terms of their dynamics (e.g., linear versus nonlinear) depending on the type of facial expression (e.g., conversational or speech movements). Wallraven and colleagues (2008), for example, used different techniques to create animations of basic emotional and more subtle conversational expressions. The authors found a recognition advantage for expressions based on natural facial motion compared to linear morphs, with a stronger effect for conversational than for emotional expressions. Cosker et al. (2010) have also reported a perceptual advantage for natural facial motion dynamics compared to linear motion, and that advantage depended on the type of facial action. Consistent with these findings, in our study linear approximations (e.g., lin1, lin2) were chosen more often for the facial expressions fear, happiness and surprise compared to the facial expression anger which contained speech movements. This suggests that, perhaps unsurprisingly, different kinds of approximations work best for different facial expressions. Testing a wide range of expressions performed by many actors could allow formulation of suggestions about which approximations best reproduce the spatio-temporal dynamics of specific facial expressions. However such an undertaking was beyond the scope of the current study.

Another aim of the experiment was to investigate which characteristic of facial motion observers used to judge the similarity between the original animation and the approximations. This will help understanding which aspect of facial motions we are most sensitive to and therefore needs to be preserved to create adequate approximations. We computed choice probabilities for three similarity measures based on facial action activation, optic flow and Gabor similarity and compared these objective measures to the pattern of perceptual similarity. We found that the similarity measure based on facial action activation best accounted for the variance in the choice behavior.

This similarity measure is based on a high-level cue and represents the similarity of face deformations over time (e.g., the way the eyebrows move in two animations). To our knowledge, this is the first demonstration that objective similarity measures can predict perceptual similarity of facial movements.

For static faces, Gabor jets which model simple and complex cells in early stages of visual processing have successfully predicted perceived similarity between facial identities (Yue et al., 2012) and facial expressions (e.g., Lyons et al., 1998; Susskind et al., 2007). Here, we adapted this image-based measure to motion stimuli. We found that Gabor similarity explained the least variance in the behavioral choice pattern among the three similarity measures, with much lower predictive power than reported for static faces (see Yue et al., 2012). Furthermore, the best fitting model did not include Gabor similarity as a predictor. There are two possible explanations for this finding. On the one hand, compared to real faces, our stimuli lack high-spatial frequency contents both in the spatial and temporal domains (e.g., freckles or skin wrinkling during expressions).This could potentially reduce the efficacy of the Gabor similarity which is based on the available frequency content of the image sequences as measured by Gabor filters. However, Gabor filters based on known properties of neurons found in early visual cortex (e.g., Jones & Palmer, 1987) remove these high spatial frequencies. In line with this, psychophysical studies found that human observers mainly use mid spatial frequencies to recognize faces (e.g., Costen, Parker, & Craw, 1996; Näsänen, 1999), neuroimaging studies have shown that low spatial frequency information play an important role in the brain responses to fearful stimuli (Vuilleumier et al 2003; Vlamings et al, 2009). It is beyond the scope of our current study to determine the extent to which high spatial frequencies may contribute to the similarity judgments for dynamic expressions. On the other hand, the low predictive performance in our experiment could be due to differences in static versus dynamic faces. In line with the latter possibility, neurophysiological and psychophysical studies (e.g., Duffy & Wurtz, 1991; Morrone, Burr, & Vaina, 1995; Wurtz, Yamasaki, Duffy, & Roy, 1990) reported that motion stimuli are processed at later stages in the visual hierarchy that are more responsive to optic flow features than to Gabor measures.

Given the importance of optic flow for the processing of natural motion stimuli (e.g., Bartels, Zeki, & Logothetis, 2008), we hypothesized that objective similarity between stimuli measured by optic flow might explain the behavioral similarity judgments we observed. We indeed found that optic flow was an important predictor of the perceptual choices. However, the contribution to the behavioral variance by optic flow was smaller than for facial action activation. This finding suggests that the overall similarity in low-level motion might capture subtle differences in face motion stimuli which are less relevant for observers' decisions than the spatio-temporal dynamics of local face parts. In the future, it would be interesting to investigate how responses of higher-level models of biological motion which combine Gabor filters and optic flow measures (e.g., Giese & Poggio, 2003) relates to human responses to facial motion.

We used animations of synthetic faces as stimuli in our study. While videos of faces capture much of the visual experience of perceiving real-life faces, it is difficult to precisely quantify the spatio-temporal information in videos, let alone to systematically manipulate this information to address the questions raised in this study. Still the question arises whether the reported results can be generalized to faces in real life. Evidence from psychophysical and neuroimaging studies investigating static (e.g., Dyck et al., 2008; Ishai, Schmidt, & Boesiger, 2005; Wilson, Loffler, & Wilkinson, 2002) and dynamic face processing (e.g., McDonnell, Breidt, & Bülthoff, 2012; Mar, Kelley, Heatherton, & Macrae, 2007; Moser et al., 2007) indicates that synthetic faces are processed by similar mechanisms as natural faces. However, contradictory results have also been reported (e.g., Han, Jiang, Humphreys, Zhou, & Cai, 2005; Moser et al., 2007). These differences in results may be due to differences in the naturalness of the synthetic face stimuli across these studies, highlighting the need to capture natural facial motions with a high degree of fidelity. As we have strived to generate avatars with motion as natural as possible, we believe that our results would generalize to real-life faces if the same tests could be run under controlled conditions. With the techniques available today, we do not expect any of our similarity measures to account better for the perceived similarity between videos than perceived similarity between our animations, since videos contain much more irrelevant information that would need to be discounted for a sensitive analysis (e.g., head movements, different backgrounds, hair).

Our results suggest that observers extract spatio-temporal characteristics of facial motion stimuli and make their judgments based on a sparse but semantically meaningful representation rather than on low-level physical properties of the stimuli. Given the social importance of facial motion, it is likely that despite the fact that observers were asked to perform a simple similarity judgment task, they automatically extracted and analyzed the semantic content of facial motion. To further test this hypothesis in a future experiment, one could use nonsense facial motion stimuli (e.g., by scrambling the frames) or inverted face motion stimuli to investigate whether image-based measures better explain the perceived similarity of such stimuli.

2.6 Conclusions

We draw three main conclusions from our study. First, our results demonstrate how exquisitely sensitive the human perceptual system is to degradations of the spatio-temporal properties of natural facial motion: observers discriminated the subtle differences between the different approximations and preferred animations containing more information about the natural facial motion dynamics. Second, the perceived similarity of an approximation depended on the type of facial expression, which shows that the use of simple approximations, such as linear interpolations, is not appropriate to reproduce all types of facial expressions. Third, our approach allowed a quantitative explanation of observers' perceptual choices revealing the importance of high-level cues in the processing of facial motion. These findings suggest that to understand facial motion processing, we need more advanced analyses than for static images, going beyond the analysis of image-based properties. These conclusions validate attempts to capture and render semantically meaningful information in facial motion. Using better approximations will open the door to in-depth studies of how humans judge and perceive natural facial motion, what information in facial motion they rely on when performing different tasks involving facial motion, and what neural mechanisms underlie the processing of these different kinds of information. We believe that such methods are essential for a systematic, quantitative analysis of the incredible amount of information that can be conveyed by facial motion and have important implications for theories and models of facial motion perception.

Acknowledgements

The project was supported by Perceptual Graphics project PAK 38 CU 149/1-1/2 funded by the Deutsche Forschungs Gemeinschaft (DFG) and EU Project EC FP7-ICT-249858 TANGO. Further, we would like to thank Mario Kleiner for his valuable input and support by implementing the motion analysis system to acquire the stimuli for this study; Prof. Martin Giese for advice on the experimental design; Dr. Stephan de la Rosa for advice on statistics; and Prof. Heinrich H. Bülthoff for support. There was no conflict of interest.

2.7 Appendix

A.1 Facial animation procedure

A.1.1 Acquiring and post-processing facial motion capture data

We captured facial movements of a non-professional female actor using a seven-cameras optical motion capture system (NaturalPoint Optitrack) running at 100Hz, and OptiTrack Expression software (version 1.8.0, NaturalPoint, Inc., Corvallis, OR, USA). The positions of 41 reflective markers (37 markers on the actor's face and 4 markers on a headband, see left image of Figure 2A) were tracked by six infra-red cameras, while an additional synchronized scene camera recorded a gray-scale video of the actor performing the facial movements (see Figure 2A).

At the beginning of the motion capture session, 30 facial actions were captured from the actor. These actions are listed in Table A.1. Although the selected facial actions were mainly based on FACS, the actor and the instructor were not certified FACS experts. The actor received verbal instructions for each facial action and was instructed to perform the movement as intensely and as clearly as possible, with as little co-activation as possible in other facial regions corresponding to other facial actions. From these recordings, we manually selected the frame displaying the maximum intensity for each of the 30 facial actions (e.g., eyebrow raising: when the eyebrows were maximally raised).

Table A.1. The 30 recorded facial actions and their semantic meaning specifying which part of the face moves and in which way.

Facial Action	Semantic	Facial Action	Semantic
1	Neutral	16	Lips open
2	Eyebrows lowered	17	Mouth open
3	Eyebrows raised	18	Mouth wide open
4	Eyes wide open	19	Lower lip down
5	Eyes squint	20	Mouth stretched
6	Eyes closed	21	Dimpler
7	Nose wrinkled	22	Smile, mouth closed
8	Upper lip up	23	Right lips up
9	Upper lip up, teeth showed	24	Left lips up
10	Right mouth corner up	25	Smile, mouth open
11	Left mouth corner up	26	Lip corners up
12	Chin up	27	Pucker
13	Lip corners down	28	Lips funnel
14	Right lip corner down	29	Lips tight
15	Left lip corner down	30	Lips pressed

The actor then performed four emotional facial expressions (anger, fear, happiness and surprise) that involved a wide range of facial motion distributed across different regions of the face (e.g., mouth, eyebrows). To induce the expressions as naturally as possible, we used a "method-acting protocol" in which the actor is verbally given a particular background scenario designed to elicit the desired facial expression (see Kaulard et al., 2012). Three of the recorded expressions (fear, happiness, and surprise) started from a neutral expression and proceeded to the target expression. For the facial expression anger, we chose a background scenario leading up to an anger expression that contained visual speech (i.e., "speak angrily to someone"). This facial expression increased the range of spatio-temporal profiles of facial motion tested in our study.

Using OptiTrack Arena Expression software, the facial motion data was post-processed as follows. First, the markers were labeled according to their position on the face. Triangulation errors were manually removed from the marke position time courses and rarely occurring gaps in time courses were filled in by cubic spline interpolation. Second, rigid head motion was removed from the motion capture data by aligning the four recorded head markers to their positions at the start of the motion capture. Third, the remaining non-rigid component of the motion data was loaded into Matlab (version R2010b, The MathWorks, Inc., Natick, MA, USA) using the MoCap Toolbox (Burger & Toiviainen, 2013), and filtered with a low pass filter (digital Butterworth filter, cut-off frequency = 10 Hz, order = 2) to reduce jitter in the marker time courses.

A.1.2 Analyzing facial motion capture data

The post-processed motion capture data for each expression were decomposed into time courses of the constituent facial actions (see Table A1). These time courses were obtained by linearly combining the marker positions of the set of static facial actions to the marker positions at each time point of the recorded expression (see Curio et al., 2006 for further details). The activation for each facial action at each time point ranged from 0 (no activation) to 1 (maximum intensity). We first identified the peak of the facial expression by summing all 30 facial action activations at each time point and selecting the frame that had the largest sum. For each facial action, we then selected sequences of 1s duration (100 frames) that contained this peak at the end of the sequence.

A.1.3 Facial motion retargeting

The time courses were transferred onto a female 3D head model designed in Poser 8 (SmithMicro, Inc., Watsonville, CA, USA). We manually altered the model using Poser's in-built animation parameters to create 30 facial action "shapes" corresponding to the 30 facial actions performed by the actor (at their maximum intensity). Figure 2B shows the facial actions "neutral" (facial action 1), "mouth open" (facial action 17) and "smile" (facial action 22) as motion capture data (middle) and the corresponding facial action shape (right). Each of the facial action shapes was exported in OBJ format from Poser into the animation software 3ds Max 2012 (Autodesk, Inc., San Rafael, CA, USA). The 3D coordinates of all the facial action shapes were in correspondence (e.g., the tip of the nose is represented by the same vertex across all shapes). This correspondence allowed us to take a weighted linear combination (i.e., morph) of the neutral action shape with all the other action shapes (sometimes referred to as weighted morphing). For example, increasing the weight of any particular action shape (e.g., mouth open) adds increasing amounts of that action shape to the neutral action shape. To synthesize a complex facial expression, the facial action shapes were weighted by their activation at each frame (time step) and combined with the neutral action shape. This combination was done in 3ds Max.

46

2.8 References

Ambadar, Z., Schooler, J. W., & Cohn, J. F. (2005). Deciphering the enigmatic face: The importace of facial dynamics in interpreting subtle facial expressions. Psychological Science, 16(5), 403–410.

Bartels, A., Zeki, S., & Logothetis, N. K. (2008). Natural vision reveals regional specialization to local motion and to contrast-invariant, global flow in the human brain. Cerebral Cortex, 18(3), 705–717. doi:10.1093/cercor/bhm107

Bernstein, L. E., Demorest, M. E., & Tucker, P. E. (2000). Speech perception without hearing. Perception & Psychophysics, 62(2), 233–252.

Bruce, V., & Young, A. W. (1986). Understanding face recognition. British Journal of Psychology London England 1953, 77(3), 305–327.

Burger, B., & Toiviainen, P. (2013). MoCap Toolbox-A Matlab toolbox for computational analysis of movement data. In R. Bresin (Ed.), Proceedings of the Sound and Music Computing Conference 2013 (pp. 172–178). Stockholm, Sweden: KTH Royal Institute of Technology.

Calder, A. J., & Young, A. W. (2005). Understanding the recognition of facial identity and facial expression. Nature Reviews Neuroscience, 6(8), 641–51. doi:10.1038/nrn1724

Cosker, D., Krumhuber, E., & Hilton, A. (2010). Perception of linear and nonlinear motion properties using a FACS validated 3D facial model. In Proceedings of the 7th Symposium on Applied Perception in Graphics and Visualization (pp. 101–108). New York, NY: ACM Press. doi:10.1145/1836248.1836268

Costen, N., Parker, D., & Craw, I. (1996). Effects of high-pass and low-pass spatial filtering on face identification. Perception & Psychophysics, 58(4), 602–612.

Cunningham, D. W., & Wallraven, C. (2009). The interaction between motion and form in expression recognition. In Proceedings of the 6th Symposium on Applied Perception in Graphics and Visualization (pp. 41–44). New York, NY: ACM Press. doi:10.1145/1620993.1621002

Curio, C., Breidt, M., Kleiner, M., Vuong, Q. C., Giese, M. A., & Bülthoff, H. H. (2006). Semantic 3D motion retargeting for facial animation. In Proceedings of the 3rd Symposium on Applied Perception in Graphics and Visualization (pp. 77–84). New York, NY: ACM Press. doi:10.1145/1140491.1140508

Duffy, C., & Wurtz, R. (1991). Sensitivity of MST Neurons to Optic Flow Stimuli. I. A Continuum of Response Selectivity to Large-Field Stimuli. Journal of Neurophysiology, 65(6), 1329–1345.

Dyck, M., Winbeck, M., Leiberg, S., Chen, Y., Gur, R. C., & Mathiak, K. (2008). Recognition profile of emotions in natural and virtual faces. PLoS ONE, 3(11), e3628. doi:10.1371/journal.pone.0003628

Ekman, P., Friesen, W. V., & Hager, J. C. (2002). The Facial Action Coding System. Salt Lake City, UT: A Human Face.

Ekman, P., & Friesen, W. V. (1978). Facial Action Coding System: A technique for the measurement of facial movement. Palo Alto, CA: Consulting Psychologists Press.

Furl, N., van Rijsbergen, N. J., Kiebel, S. J., Friston, K. J., Treves, A., & Dolan, R. J. (2010). Modulation of Perception and Brain Activity by Predictable Trajectories of Facial Expressions. Cerebral Cortex, 20(3), 694–703. doi:10.1093/cercor/bhp140

Giese, M. A., & Poggio, T. (2003). Neural mechanisms for the recognition of biological movements. Nature Reviews Neuroscience, 4(3), 179–192. doi:10.1038/nrn1057

Han, S., Jiang, Y., Humphreys, G. W., Zhou, T., & Cai, P. (2005). Distinct neural substrates for the perception of real and virtual visual worlds. NeuroImage, 24(3), 928–935. doi:10.1016/j.neuroimage.2004.09.046

Haxby, J. V., Hoffman, E. A., & Gobbini, M. I. (2002). Human neural systems for face recognition and social communication. Biological psychiatry, 51(1), 59–67.

Hoerl, A. E., & Kennard, R. W. (1970). Ridge regression: Biased estimation for nonorthogonal problems. Technometrics, 12(1), 55–67.

Horn, B. K. P., & Schunck, B. G. (1981). Determining optical flow. Artificial Intelligence, 17(1), 185–203. doi:10.1016/0004-3702(81)90024-2

Ishai, A., Schmidt, C. F., & Boesiger, P. (2005). Face perception is mediated by a distributed cortical network. Brain Research Bulletin, 67(1), 87–93. doi:10.1016/j.brainresbull.2005.05.027

Jack, R. E., Garrod, O. G. B., Yu, H., Caldara, R., & Schyns, P. G. (2012). Facial expressions of emotion are not culturally universal. Proceedings of the National Academy of Sciences, 109(19), 7241–7244. doi:10.1073/pnas.1200155109

Jones, J. P., & Palmer, L. A. (1987). An evaluation of the two-dimensional Gabor filter model of simple receptive fields in cat striate cortex. Journal of Neurophysiology, 58(6), 1233–1258.

Kamachi, M., Bruce, V., Mukaida, S., Gyoba, J., Yoshikawa, S., & Akamatsu, S. (2001). Dynamic properties influence the perception of facial expressions. Perception, 30, 875–887. doi:10.1068/p3131

Kaulard, K., Cunningham, D. W., Bülthoff, H. H., & Wallraven, C. (2012). The MPI Facial Expression Database — A Validated Database of Emotional and Conversational Facial Expressions. PLoS ONE, 7(3), e32321. doi:10.1371/journal.pone.0032321

Kleiner, M. (2010). Visual stimulus timing precision in Psychtoolbox-3: Tests, pitfalls and solutions. Perception, 39(ECVP Abstract Supplement), 189.

Krumhuber, E. G., Kappas, A., & Manstead, A. S. R. (2013). Effects of Dynamic Aspects of Facial Expressions: A Review. Emotion Review, 5(1), 41–46. doi:10.1177/1754073912451349

Ku, J., Jang, H., Kim, K., Kim, J., Park, S., Lee, J., ... Kim, S. (2005). Experimental results of affective valence and arousal to avatar's facial expressions. CyberPsychology & Behavior, 8(5), 493–503.

LaBar, K. S., Crupain, M. J., Voyvodic, J. T., & McCarthy, G. (2003). Dynamic perception of facial affect and identity in the human brain. Cerebral Cortex, 13(10), 1023–1033.

Lades, M., Vorbrüggen, J. C., Buhmann, J., Lange, J., von der Malsburg, C., Würtz, R. P., & Konen, W. (1993). Distortion invariant object recognition in the dynamic link architecture. IEEE Transactions on Computers, 42(3), 300–311.

Luce, R. D. (1959). Individual Choice Behavior: A Theoretical Analysis. New York, NY: John Wiley and sons.

Lyons, M., Akamatsu, S., Kamachi, M., & Gyoba, J. (1998). Coding facial expressions with Gabor wavelets. In Proceedings of the 3rd International Conference on Automatic Face and Gesture Recognition (pp. 200–205). Washington, DC: IEEE Computer Society.

Mar, R. A., Kelley, W. M., Heatherton, T. F., & Macrae, C. N. (2007). Detecting agency from the biological motion of veridical vs animated agents. Social Cognitive and Affective Neuroscience, 2(3), 199–205. doi:10.1093/scan/nsm011

McDonnell, R., Breidt, M., & Bülthoff, H. H. (2012). Render me real? Investigating the Effect of Render Style on the Perception of Animated Virtual Humans. ACM Transactions on Graphics, 31(4), 91.

Morrone, M. C., Burr, D. C., & Vaina, L. M. (1995). Two stages of visual processing for radial and circular motion. Nature, 376, 507–509.

Moser, E., Derntl, B., Robinson, S., Fink, B., Gur, R. C., & Grammer, K. (2007). Amygdala activation at 3T in response to human and avatar facial expressions of emotions. Journal of Neuroscience Methods, 161(1), 126–133. doi:10.1016/j.jneumeth.2006.10.016

Näsänen, R. (1999). Spatial frequency bandwidth used in the recognition of facial images. Vision research, 39(23), 3824–33.

Pollick, F. E., Hill, H., Calder, A. J., & Paterson, H. (2003). Recognising facial expression from spatially and temporally modified movements. Perception, 32(7), 813–826. doi:10.1068/p3319

Rhodes, G. (1988). Looking at faces: First-order and second-order features as determinants of facial appearance. Perception, 17, 43–63.

Roesch, E. B., Tamarit, L., Reveret, L., Grandjean, D., Sander, D., & Scherer, K. R. (2011). FACSGen: A tool to synthesize emotional facial expressions through systematic manipulation of facial action units. Journal of Nonverbal Behavior, 35(1), 1–16. doi:10.1007/s10919-010-0095-9

Rosenblum, L. D., Yakel, D. A., Baseer, N., Panchal, A., Nodarse, B. C., & Niehus, R. P. (2002). Visual speech information for face recognition. Perception & Psychophysics, 64(2), 220–229.

Sarkheil, P., Goebel, R., Schneider, F., & Mathiak, K. (2012). Emotion unfolded by motion: a role for parietal lobe in decoding dynamic facial expressions. Social Cognitive and Affective Neuroscience. doi:10.1093/scan/nss092

Sato, W., & Yoshikawa, S. (2007). Enhanced Experience of Emotional Arousal in Response to Dynamic Facial Expressions. Journal of Nonverbal Behavior, 31(2), 119–135. doi:10.1007/s10919-007-0025-7

Steyvers, M., & Busey, T. (2000). Predicting Similarity Ratings to Faces using Physical Descriptions. In M. Wenger & J. Townsend (Eds.), Computational, geometric, and process perspectives on facial cognition: Contexts and challenges (pp. 115–146). Lawrence Erlbaum Associates.

Susskind, J. M., Littlewort, G., Bartlett, M. S., Movellan, J., & Anderson, A. K. (2007). Human and computer recognition of facial expressions of emotion. Neuropsychologia, 45(1), 152–162. doi:10.1016/j.neuropsychologia.2006.05.001

Tibshirani, R. (1996). Regression shrinkage and selection via the lasso. Journal of the Royal Statistical Society. Series B (Methodological), 58(1), 267–288.

Vlamings, P. H. J. M., Goffaux, V., & Kemner, C. (2009). Is the early modulation of brain activity by fearful facial expressions primarily mediated by coarse low spatial frequency information? Journal of Vision, 9(5), 1–13.

Vuilleumier, P., Armony, J. L., Driver, J., & Dolan, R. J. (2003). Distinct spatial frequency sensitivities for processing faces and emotional expressions. Nature Neuroscience, 6(6), 624–631.

Wallraven, C., Breidt, M., Cunningham, D. W., & Bülthoff, H. H. (2008). Evaluating the perceptual realism of animated facial expressions. ACM Transactions on Applied Perception, 4(4), 1–20. doi:10.1145/1278760.1278764

Wilson, H. R., Loffler, G., & Wilkinson, F. (2002). Synthetic faces, face cubes, and the geometry of face space. Vision Research, 42(27), 2909–2923.

Wurtz, R., Yamasaki, D., Duffy, C. J., & Roy, J.-P. (1990). Functional specialization for visual motion processing in primate cerebral cortex. Cold Spring Harbor Symposia on Quantitative Biology, 55, 717–727.

Xu, X., & Biederman, I. (2010). Loci of the release from fMRI adaptation for changes in facial expression, identity, and viewpoint. Journal of Vision, 10, 1–13. doi:10.1167/10.14.36.Introduction

Yu, H., Garrod, O. G. B., & Schyns, P. G. (2012). Perception-driven facial expression synthesis. Computers & Graphics, 36(3), 152–162. doi:10.1016/j.cag.2011.12.002

Yue, X., Biederman, I., Mangini, M. C., von der Malsburg, C., & Amir, O. (2012). Predicting the psychophysical similarity of faces and non-face complex shapes by image-based measures. Vision Research, 55, 41–46. doi:10.1016/j.visres.2011.12.012

Zou, H., & Hastie, T. (2005). Regularization and variable selection via the elastic net. Journal of the Royal Statistical Society: Series B (Statistical Methodology), 67(2), 301–320. doi:10.1111/j.1467-9868.2005.00503.x

3 Identity information in facial motion varies with the type of facial movement

3.1 Abstract

Several lines of evidence have shown that idiosyncratic facial movements can convey information about identity in addition to facial form (Hill & Johnston, 2001; Knappmeyer, Thornton, & Bülthoff, 2003; Lander, Chuang, & Wickham, 2006; Rosenblum et al., 2002), yet the exact role of facial motion as a cue for identity is still unclear (O'Toole, Roark, & Abdi, 2002). In particular, it is not known which facial movements are idiosyncratic, and how efficiently the face perception system extracts identity information from these facial movements. Here, we hypothesize that the amount of identity information and humans' sensitivity to this information varies with the type of facial movement. First, we assessed human observers' sensitivity to identity information in different types of facial movements. To this end, we recorded four different actors performing facial movements in three social contexts: (1) emotional (e.g., anger), (2) emotional in a social interaction (e.g., being angry at someone) and (3) social interaction (e.g., saying goodbye to someone). To separate form from motion cues, we used a recent facial motion capture and animation system (Dobs et al., 2014) and animated a single avatar head with the recorded nonrigid facial movements from these four actors. Using a delayed matching-to-sample task, we tested in which context human observers can match the identity of unfamiliar actors based only on their facial motion. Observers were able to match the identity across emotional facial movements occurring in a social interaction, but not across basic emotional facial expressions. Sensitivity was highest across non-emotional, speech-related movements occurring in a social interaction. Second, we quantified spatio-temporal information (e.g., amount of eyebrow raise) of the recorded facial movements and built model observers processing this measure. These model observers showed higher sensitivity than our human observers, but importantly, they showed the same pattern of performance across contexts. Thus, our findings reveal (i) that human observers cannot recognize unfamiliar persons from the way they perform basic emotional facial expressions even though these expressions do contain some identity information, and (ii) that such recognition is possible from conversational and speech-related movements which contain more identity information. We hypothesize that these differences are due to the constraints under which these movements are executed: basic emotions are performed quite stereotypically, whereas conversational and speech-related movements are performed more idiosyncratically.

3.2 Introduction

In real life our faces are constantly moving, expressing our state of mind and enabling us to socially interact with others. Humans can quickly extract and interpret the facial information conveyed by facial movements. Moreover, accurate interpretation of the social signals may not require knowledge of the person's identity. Indeed, common models of face perception assume that the processing of facial motion is largely independent of processing facial identity (Bruce & Young, 1986; but see also Calder & Young, 2005; Haxby, Hoffman, & Gobbini, 2000; Schweinberger & Soukup, 1998). However, previous studies have shown that characteristic facial movements may carry cues about identity which humans can use to categorize or recognize persons (Hill & Johnston, 2001; Knappmeyer et al., 2003; Lander et al., 2006; Lander & Chuang, 2005), suggesting a stronger interaction between the processing of facial motion and identity than previously assumed. To date, the exact role of facial motion as a cue for identity is still under debate (O'Toole et al., 2002). In particular, which facial movements are idiosyncratic, and when and how the face perception system extracts identity information from these facial movements, are still unanswered questions.

Facial movements occur in multiple social contexts and differ in various aspects. For example, they can express pure emotions or non-emotional communicative intentions, they can occur in solitary or interpersonal contexts, among many others. Previous research on basic emotional facial expressions (typically defined as anger, disgust, fear, happiness, sadness and surprise) has suggested that these ecologically salient facial movements are 'universal', that is, they are performed in a stereotypical manner and can be recognized across many cultures (Ekman, 1992; Ekman, Sorenson, & Friesen, 1969; but see also Jack, Garrod, Yu, Caldara, & Schyns, 2012; Russell, 1994; Tomkins, 1962). If so, one would expect individual differences in performing the same facial expression to be small compared to differences between facial expressions. Indeed, computational analyses on emotional facial expressions revealed that their discriminative information minimally overlap, suggesting that emotional facial expressions developed such that they can be efficiently recognized (Schyns, Petro, & Smith, 2009; Smith, Cottrell, Gosselin, & Schyns, 2005). Moreover, a recent study in the field of computer vision reported that recorded emotional facial movements did not contain sufficient information for identity recognition (Benedikt, Cosker, Rosin, & Marshall, 2010).

Recently, the perception of facial movements beyond the basic emotional facial expressions have started to attract researchers' attention (Ambadar, Schooler, & Cohn, 2005; Cunningham & Wallraven, 2009; Gill, Garrod, Jack, & Schyns, 2014; Kaulard, Cunningham, Bülthoff, & Wallraven, 2012; Rosenblum et al., 2002). Compared to emotional facial expression, these facial movements are more subtle and complex and may thus be performed more idiosyncratically. In agreement with this idea, studies have shown that facial speech movements can provide identity information for human(Rosenblum et al., 2002) and computer recognition (Benedikt et al., 2010; Luettin, Thacker, & Beet, 1996). Given these results, we hypothesize that the amount of identity information contained in facial motion depends on the type of facial movement: Emotional facial expressions may be performed rather stereotypically and thus contain little identity information whereas less constrained conversational and speech-related movements may be performed more idiosyncratically and contain more identity information.

Recent neuroimaging studies have reported a dissociation between processing emotional versus neutral or speech-related (non-emotional) facial movements (Foley, Rippon, Thai, Longe, & Senior, 2012; Harris, Young, & Andrews, 2014) suggesting separate processing routes for different types of facial movements. Moreover, compared to emotional facial expressions, studies found that more complex facial expressions occurring in social interactions (e.g., agreement, confusion) are easier to recognize if presented dynamically (Cunningham & Wallraven, 2009; Kaulard et al., 2012). This suggests that information encoded in the facial movements is processed by the brain and is useful for recognizing such expressions. If these expressions are less stereotypical, can identity information also be extracted from the facial motion during this processing? Along these lines, one could expect that basic emotional facial expressions are processed primarily with respect to their emotional content (e.g., a fearful face signals fast approaching danger), while identity information may be extracted during the processing of more complex and subtle facial movements occurring in a social interaction. Thus, determining whether identity judgments depend on the type of facial movement provides an opportunity to understand the more general function of facial motion in identity perception.

To study how different types of facial movements affect identity perception, it is necessary to consider two separate components contributing to the perception of identity from facial motion: First, the face motion as signal containing spatio-temporal information and second, the observer as a decoder of this information. For example, a smaller sensitivity to identity information in emotional than conversational facial expressions could be due to less identity information in emotional facial movements (transmitter-based factor) or could be due to differences in decoding these two types of facial expressions (observer-based factor; e.g., human biases to focus on different parts of the face). Indeed, previous studies have suggested differences in social attention elicited by different types of facial movements (Lander & Bruce, 2003; Schweinberger & Soukup, 1998; Snow, Lannen, O'Toole, & Abdi, 2002). One widely used approach to assess whether behavioral effects are caused by differences in stimuli is to correlate human behavior with the behavior of model observers based on specific characteristics of the stimuli (Näsänen, 1999; Sato & Yoshikawa, 2007; Sekuler, Gaspar, Gold, & Bennett, 2004; Smith et al., 2005). In the case of facial motion stimuli, however, the spatio-temporal information conveyed by facial movements is rich and complex, making it difficult to extract meaningful stimulus characteristics.

Another major challenge when investigating identity information in facial motion is to disentangle facial motion from facial form information. While former studies have employed as stimuli movies of faces presented in suboptimal viewing conditions to degrade facial form information (Lander et al., 2006; Lander & Chuang, 2005), more recent studies have used synthetic faces animated by motion-capture data (Hill & Johnston, 2001; Knappmeyer et al., 2003). Although the latter approach allows for a separation of facial form and motion cues, it is still technically challenging to quantify and systematically analyze the underlying temporal characteristics of these stimuli. One way to isolate and quantify meaningful cues in complex facial movements is to capture spatio-temporal properties of local facial actions (Ekman & Friesen, 1976). A facial movement can then be represented as a set of time courses which capture the changes over time in the magnitude of activation of local facial regions (e.g., the amount of eyebrow raising in the facial expression surprise). To implement this approach, Curio and colleagues have developed a system to extract meaningful spatio-temporal information from natural facial movement data by decomposing motion-capture data into time courses of facial action activation (Curio et al., 2006). This technique allows for analyzing and interpreting spatio-temporal characteristics of facial movements while separating facial motion from facial form information. Importantly, a recent study has suggested that human observers use this sparse but meaningful representation to process facial motion (Dobs et al., 2014). Moreover, it is feasible to build model observers that process these spatio-temporal characteristics, which allows obtaining an upper bound of transmitter-based performance (i.e., excluding human biases and other sources of noisy performance). Thus, such a facial animation system would offer a means to directly compare model observer performance, which contains only transmitter-based effects, to human performance, which contains both observer and transmitter effects.

In the current study, we aimed to replicate previous findings demonstrating the use of spatio-temporal information in facial movements for identity perception, and to assess whether the amount of this information varies across the social context in which the facial movements were recorded. We hypothesized that the less stereotypical facial expressions are, the more identity information they would convey. To this end, we captured from four different actors individual facial movements elicited by a method-acting protocol (see Kaulard et al., 2012) in three social contexts: (1) "emotional" (e.g., anger), (2) "emotional in social interaction" (e.g., being angry at someone) and (3) "social interaction" (e.g., saying goodbye to someone). We used the facial animation technique developed by Curio and colleagues (2006) to animate one single avatar head with these facial movements (Curio et al., 2006; Dobs et al., 2014). In a within-subject design, observers performed identity judgments on the movements captured in each of the three social contexts. For each context (e.g., emotional), observers were presented with a sample facial movement X (e.g., anger) and then with two "match" facial movements of another kind (e.g., disgust). Their task was to select the match stimulus that had been recorded from the same actor as the sample stimulus (i.e., they performed a matching-to-sample task about the identity of the actor from which the movement was recorded). To anticipate from our results, observers were able to match actor identities in the latter two contexts (emotional in social interaction and the social interaction context), but not in the emotional context, and showed highest sensitivity for the social interaction context. Moreover, model observers based on meaningful spatio-temporal characteristics of facial movements (e.g., the amount of eyebrow raising) showed the same trend, suggesting that these effects are transmitter-based rather than observer-based. Our results are the first to systematically investigate how sensitive human observers are to identity information across different types of facial movements. They also confirm our hypothesis that the less stereotypical facial movements are, the more identity information they contain.

3.3 Methods

Participants

Fourteen participants (6 female; mean age: 30.2 ± 7.5 years) were recruited from the subject database of the Max Planck Institute for Biological Cybernetics, Tübingen, Germany, and participated in the experiment. All observers were naive to the purpose of the experiment and had normal or corrected-to-normal vision. They provided informed written consent before the experiment began and filled out a post-questionnaire at the end of the experiment. The study was conducted in accordance to the Declaration of Helsinki.

Stimuli and display

To create animations of facial movements, which were identical in facial form but differed in facial motion, we used a motion-retargeting and facial animation procedure (Fig. 1). The animation procedure was as follows. First, we motion-recorded 12 different facial movements of four non-professional female actors using a marker-based optical motion capture system (for details see Dobs et al., 2014). All facial movements were recorded using a method-acting protocol in which the actor was verbally given a particular background scenario designed to elicit the desired facial movements (see Kaulard et al., 2012). Actors were instructed to begin each facial movement with a neutral expression. The 12 facial movements were categorized into three different contexts (four movements each) in which they normally occur: "emotional" (i.e., emotional facial expressions), "emotional in social interaction" (i.e., emotional and facial speech movements occurring in a social interaction) or "social interaction" (i.e., facial speech movements occurring in a social interaction without emotional content). Details

56

for each facial movement of the three contexts and its corresponding exemplary scenario are listed in Table 1. Second, one single female avatar face was manually designed in Poser 8 (SmithMicro, Inc., Watsonville, CA, USA) and animated by each of the motion-recorded facial movements. To this end, we used a system that decomposes the recorded motion data into time-courses of meaningful facial actions (Curio et al., 2006) which were used to animate the avatar model with corresponding facial actions. This motion-retargeting procedure gave us an identity-independent representation of spatio-temporal facial motion information and hence ensuring that animations were independent of an actor's facial form (i.e., spatial placement of tracking markers in the face). Finally, the 48 animations were rendered as Quicktime movies of 3.5 s duration (300 x 400 pixels, Codec H.264, 60Hz) in 3ds Max 2012 (Autodesk, Inc., San Rafael, CA, USA).

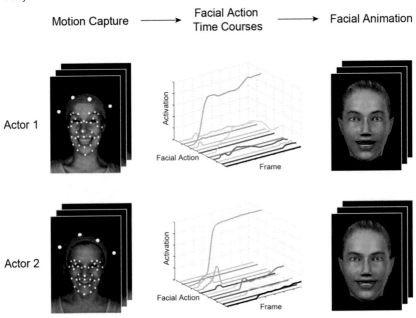

Figure 1. Schematic overview of the facial animation procedure, shown for the facial expression happiness. In the first step, motion capture data of a facial movement (here, facial expression happiness) is recorded from different actors (left). In the second step, the facial animation system decomposes the motion capture data of the facial movement into time courses of facial action activation (middle). In the last step, the time courses of facial action activation are used to animate a single semantically matched 3D face model (right).

Stimuli were presented and responses recorded using PsychToolbox 3 for Matlab (http://www.psychtoolbox.org) (Kleiner, 2010). Observers were seated approximately 60 cm from a Dell 2407WFP monitor (24 inch screen diagonal size, 1920 x 1200 pixel resolution; 60Hz refresh rate). Animation stimuli were scaled to a size of 9° x 12°.

Table 1. Overview of the 12 recorded facial movements, their contexts and exemplary scenarios.

Context	Facial movement label	Exemplary scenario
Emotional	Anger	You are very hungry and realize that someone took the food which you were looking forward to all day.
	Disgust	After you come home from a journey, you find molded food in your fridge.
	Fear	While cycling downhill, you suddenly realize that your brakes do not work.
	Happiness	You are laughing about a funny scene in a movie.
Emotional in interaction	Anger_Soc	You are yelling at someone because he took your food without asking.
	Disgust_Soc	You tell a friend how disgusting you think molded food is.
	Fear_Soc	You are very frightened because you saw something in the forest at night and you try to warn a friend.
	Happiness_Soc	You tell a friend about an exam that you just passed and that you are very happy about.
Interaction	Introduction_Casual	You introduce yourself to someone on a party.
	Introduction_Professional	You introduce yourself to your prospective employer.
	Farewell_Casual	You say goodbye to a friend on a party.
	Farewell_Professional	At the end of a job interview, you say goodbye to your prospective employer.

Design and procedure

To test the effect of social context on observers' ability to discriminate identities based on their facial movements, we had them perform a delayed match-to-sample task on the dynamic face stimuli for each of the three contexts tested in three separate experiments. In each experiment (e.g., emotional context), observers first watched an animation of one of the four facial movements (e.g., happiness) as sample, followed by two animations displaying a different facial movement (e.g., disgust) as matching stimuli. One of the matching stimuli was performed by the same actor as the sample, while the distractor stimulus was performed by another actor. Observers were asked to choose which of the two matching stimuli was performed by the same actor as the sample. The order of experiments (i.e., social contexts) was randomized across observers. For each experiment and observer, 48 of all 144 possible combinations of actors and facial movements (recorded in this context) were randomly selected as trials. The combinations of actors and facial movements were pseudorandomized such that each of the 12 possible actor combinations (e.g., actor 1 as sample, actor 2 as distractor) and each of the 12 facial movement combinations (e.g., happiness as sample, disgust as matches) were shown four times. The presentation of the distractor on the left or right side of the screen was counter-balanced across trials.

Figure 2 depicts the trial procedure exemplarily shown for the emotional context. All trials began with a white fixation cross on a black background shown for 1 s at the center of the screen, followed by the sample stimulus. After the animation, a black screen appeared for 0.5 s, followed by two matching animations presented side-by-side, 6.7° to the left and right of fixation. Observers could indicate their readiness to respond by pressing any key on a standard computer keyboard during the trial, which caused the response screen to appear. If they did not respond, the sequence of animation, black screen and two animations was repeated up to a maximum of three presentations before the response screen appeared. The response screen showed the question "Which of the two facial motions has been captured from the same actor as the first one?". Observers pressed the left or right cursor arrow key to choose the corresponding animation. The response screen remained until observers responded. No feedback was provided. Observers could take up to three self-timed breaks after every 12 trials within an experiment and two breaks up to 15 minutes between experiments. Each experiment lasted approximately 35-45 minutes for a total duration of 120-160 minutes.

Prior to the experiments, we briefly familiarized observers with the facial animations and the four different actors by presenting them the facial movement "surprise" of each actor which was not used in the experimental session. Each facial movement was animated on the same avatar as used in the actual experiments. For each observer, the presentation order of actors was randomized. After watching the facial expression up to five times, observers had to answer two identity-related questions about the actor (e.g., "How happy is this person?"). The questions were intended to get observers acquainted with the concept that different identities are animated on the same facial structure. The introduction lasted about 10 minutes.

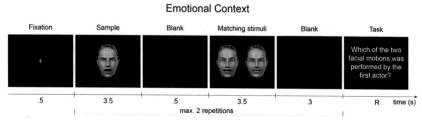

Figure 2. The trial procedure of the experiment.

Model Observer

To test whether the behavioral sensitivity could be predicted by the facial movement information contained in the activity of facial actions (see Fig. 1), we built model observers corresponding to the human observers. For each of the three experimental contexts, a model observer ran the same experiment as each of the fourteen human observers using the same stimulus randomization. Note that each human observer was presented with a different random set of trials (see Design and procedure). Thus, a model observer simulating a single observer was presented with the same stimuli as those presented to the human observer. For each experimental context and each trial, we computed the model observer's choices as follows. First, we measured the similarity in terms of facial action activation between the two matches a and b and the sample stimuli x (e.g., between 'happiness' of actor 1 and 'anger' of actor 1 and 2, respectively). For two facial movements a and x, we computed the distance between them as the Euclidean distance between the mean activation of facial actions:

$$d_{FA}(a,b) = \sqrt{\sum_{i=1}^{n}(\bar{a}_i - \bar{b}_i)^2} \quad , \tag{1}$$

where $n = 30$ is the number of facial actions used and a_i represents the mean activation of facial action i in facial movement a across time (i.e., each video clip was 3.5 s with 60 Hz = 210 frames). Second, we used Luce's choice rule to compute the probability for a model observer to choose facial movement *a* given the two matches *a* and *b* and sample *x* (Luce, 1961). This choice rule has already been used successfully in other studies to predict the choice probability in a delayed match-to-sample task using facial animations (Dobs et al., 2014). According to Luce's choice rule, the probability of choosing facial movement *a* (response r_a) given matches *a* and *b* and sample *x* can be expressed as:

$$P(r_a|x) = 1 - \frac{d_{FA}(a,x)}{d_{FA}(a,x) + d_{FA}(b,x)} \quad , \tag{2}$$

where *d(a,x)* is the similarity between facial movement *a* and the sample *x*, and *d(b,x)* is the corresponding similarity between facial movement *b* and the sample *x* (see eq. 1). Third, for each trial, we simulated a model observer's choice by comparing the choice probability *P(ra/x)* with 0.5 (i.e., *P(ra/x)* > 0.5 indicates the choice of match *a*, whereas *P(ra/x)* <= 0.5 indicates choice of match *b*). Note that this step function does not take noise into account. While adding noise to the probabilities would simulate human behavior more realistically, here we aimed at obtaining an upper bound of transmitter-based performance (i.e., excluding human biases and other sources of noisy performance).

Behavioral and model observer's data analyses
To assess whether behavioral sensitivity to identity information differed for the three experimental contexts, we calculated observers' sensitivity (d' value) in each experimental context. We used the differencing rule for match-to-sample tasks to calculate d' which assumes that observers compare each of the matches *a* and *b* with the sample *x* and base their decision on these two comparisons (Macmillan & Creelman, 2004). We applied the same formula to calculate d' for each model observer simulation. To assess whether sensitivity was significantly different from chance we compared sensitivity to chance using t-tests. The sensitivity data for each experimental context, for each kind of observer, was then submitted to a one-way repeated-measures analysis of variance (ANOVA). We then compared the effect of social context between the two types of observers using a two-way mixed measures ANOVA. To further test whether similarity in facial action activation could predict the behavioral choices, we correlated the sensitivity obtained from the model observer analyses with the behavioral sensitivity using Pearson's correlation coefficient.

3.4 Results

Human behavioral data

Here, we tested human observers' sensitivity to identity information in facial movements across three social contexts. Analysis of sensitivity (d') showed that observers were able to discriminate identities based on facial motion, and that their sensitivity depended on the context (Fig. 3). Sensitivity was significantly different from chance for stimuli recorded in contexts of social interaction (INT; d' mean and SEM: 1.64 ± 0.13; percentage correct: 68%; $t(13) = 12.35$, $p < 0.0001$; t-tests calculated on d' data) and emotional interactions (EMO_INT; d' mean and SEM: 0.77 ± 0.16; percentage correct: 57%; $t(13) = 4.66$, $p < 0.0001$), while sensitivity for the stimuli recorded in the emotional context was not different from chance level (EMO; d' mean and SEM: 0.13 ± 0.21; percentage correct: 50%; $t(13) = 0.61$, $p > 0.5$). The one-way repeated-measures ANOVA revealed a main effect of context ($F(2,26) = 18.59$, $p < 0.0001$, $\eta^2 = 0.49$) suggesting that sensitivity differed across contexts. A Lilliefors test on the residuals of the ANOVA was not significant ($p > 0.1$) and thus confirmed the suitability of parametric analyses for the sensitivity data. Bonferroni corrected post-hoc comparisons showed that sensitivity was highest for the social interaction context (INT > EMO: $t(13) = -6.07$, $p < 0.0001$, *Cohen's d* = 2.26; INT > EMO_INT: $t(13) = -3.51$, $p < 0.01$, *Cohen's d* = 1.56) and smallest for the emotional context (EMO < EMO_INT: $t(13) = -2.56$, $p < 0.05$, *Cohen's d* = 0.89). These results suggest that the less stereotypical facial movements are, the more identity information can be extracted from these facial movements.

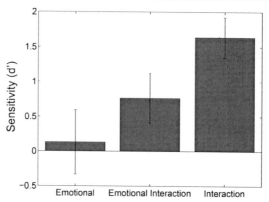

Figure 3. Behavioral results. Mean sensitivity (d') across observers (n = 14) as a function of context. A sensitivity of 0 indicates chance level. Error bars indicate 95% confidence interval (CI).

Model observer behavioral data

To assess whether the differences in human observers' sensitivity we found were due to different amounts of identity information across social contexts (transmitter-based effect) or due to different processing strategies across social contexts (observer-based effect), we simulated model observers based on the spatio-temporal characteristics of facial movements. Figure 4 shows the mean d' values obtained from the model observer analyses. Visual comparison between the behavioral sensitivity (Fig. 3) and the sensitivity of model observers reveals two aspects: first, model observers show higher sensitivity than human observers, second, model observers show a similar pattern of sensitivity for the three experimental contexts. The mean sensitivity for model observers was above chance level in all social contexts (EMO: d' mean and SEM: 1.18 ± 0.09; percentage correct: 61%; $t(13) = 13.60$, $p < 0.0001$; EMO_INT: d' mean and SEM: 1.69 ± 0.05; percentage correct: 69%; $t(13) = 31.45$, $p < 0.0001$; INT: d' mean and SEM: 2.22 ± 0.06; percentage correct: 78%; $t(13) = 39.31$, $p < 0.0001$). As for behavioral sensitivity, the sensitivity was smallest in the emotional context (EMO < EMO_INT: $t(13)$ = −4.35, $p < 0.001$, *Cohen's d* = 1.91; EMO < INT: $t(13) = -11.35$, $p < 0.0001$, *Cohen's d* = 3.83; corrected for multiple comparisons), followed by the emotional-in-social-interaction context and largest for the interactional context (INT > EMO_INT: $t(13)$ = 6.18, $p < 0.0001$, *Cohen's d* = 2.58). A mixed measures ANOVA, with social context as within factor and observer type as between subjects factor, showed a significant main effect of social context ($F(2,52) = 67.16$, $p < 0.0001$, $\eta^2 = 0.40$) and of observer type ($F(1,26) = 45.73$, $p < 0.0001$, $\eta^2 = 0.26$) but no significant interaction ($F(2,52) = 1.59$, $p > 0.2$, $\eta^2 = 0.01$). These results suggest that similarity in terms of facial action activation carries identity information which model observers can use to discriminate identities; and importantly, the amount of this information depends on the context, generating a performance pattern similar to that found in real human observers.

To assess whether the sensitivity of each observer could be predicted from the performance of the model observers performing the same trials, we correlated the d' values obtained from observers with the corresponding d' values obtained from the model observers. We found that in none of the three experimental contexts the performance of model observers could predict the variability in behavioral sensitivity (EMO: $r = -0.20$, $p > 0.4$; EMO_INT: $r = -0.04$, $p > 0.8$; INT: $r = 0.45$, $p > 0.1$). These results show that the model observer analysis failed to predict the variance in the behavioral sensitivity for each context, suggesting that this measurement does not drive individual differences in observer performance.

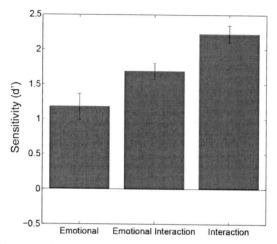

Figure 4. Model observer analysis. Mean sensitivity (d') across model observers corresponding to each observer (n = 14) as a function of context. A sensitivity of 0 indicates chance level. Error bars indicate 95% confidence interval (CI).

3.5 Discussion

Accumulating evidence suggests that identity information is not only represented in static features of a face but also in idiosyncratic facial movements (Hill & Johnston, 2001; Knappmeyer et al., 2003; Rosenblum et al., 2002; see O'Toole et al., 2002 for a review). Using a form-independent motion retargeting system, our results replicated previous studies by showing that human observers were able to match identities solely based on facial motion dynamics. However, while most studies investigating identity information in facial motion focused on a particular type of facial motion (e.g., "joke telling"; Hill & Johnston, 2001), we used facial movements elicited by three social contexts differing in various aspects, namely in the presence of interaction (i.e., solitary versus interpersonal), emotion and facial speech. We thus extend previous findings by addressing the question how different types of facial movements occurring in different social contexts affect the perception of identity from facial motion. We first demonstrated that observers are able to match the identity across emotional facial movements occurring in a social interaction, but not across purely emotional facial expressions (i.e., these did not occur in a social interaction context). Moreover, we found the highest sensitivity to identity information in non-emotional speech-related movements occurring in a social interaction. Finally, comparisons between model observers and human observers revealed similar performance patterns, suggesting that these differences in sensitivity between social contexts are due to spatio-temporal characteristics of facial movements (transmitter-based), rather than differences in processing these facial movements (observer-based). Thus, our results contribute to the understanding of the function of facial motion in identity perception by showing that the less stereotypical facial movements are, the more identity information is encoded in these facial movements.

The investigation of identity perception based on facial motion requires the consideration of two aspects of perception: first, the transmission of motion information by a facial movement (transmitter-based) and second, the processing of this information by observers (observer-based). By varying the social context, we did not only change the information conveyed by facial expressions, but we might also have influenced the use of this information by observers. Studies comparing model observers with human observers have indeed suggested that human observers show different biases in processing different types of facial expressions (Smith et al., 2005). To assess whether differences in identity matching performance between the three social contexts were solely due to differences in the amount of identity information or could also be explained by different processing strategies, we ran model observer analyses based on spatio-temporal feature descriptors of facial motion (e.g., the average amount of eyebrow raise during a facial movement). Model observers showed similar differences in sensitivity between social contexts as human observers, suggesting that the differences in human observers' sensitivity are transmitter-based rather than observer-based.

However, the performance of model observers could not explain individual differences in sensitivity within social contexts. This finding suggests that individual differences in human biases (e.g., processing strategies, such as focusing on the eye region) as well as behavioral noise (e.g., lack of concentration) may have contributed to individual differences in sensitivity. Also, sensitivity of model observers was generally higher than for human observers. Both findings are explainable by one or more of the following hypotheses: human observers may not be able to employ all available identity information contained in facial motion; they may suffer from imperfect attention to a degree that differs across participants; they may use additional decoding strategies when processing facial movements that are not optimal in this task; and our stimuli may not have been able to display in a perceptible form all of the identity information contained in the facial motion data. Further research is needed to more fully understand the influence of processing strategies on the perception of identity information in facial motion.

Facial movements can convey only emotional and communicative cues, or combine both types of information. For purely emotional facial expressions, one hypothesis is that in order to recognize these evolutionary salient signals efficiently, emotional facial expressions evolved such that they maintained stereotyped appearance. Indeed, computational analyses of the six basic facial expressions (e.g., happiness, anger) suggested that these facial expressions evolved as highly discriminative social signals (Schyns et al., 2009; Smith et al., 2005). If so, individual differences in performing these facial expressions should be small. In contrast, facial movements occurring in everyday social interactions are much more subtle and complex. Moreover, studies revealed that humans process the dynamics of these facial movements (Ambadar et al., 2005; Cunningham & Wallraven, 2009; Kaulard et al., 2012). We thus hypothesized that facial movements occurring in social interactions are performed less stereotypically than emotional facial expressions. Indeed, our results revealed that the more communicative intensions facial movements conveyed, the more identity information they contained.

In addition to emotional facial movements occurring in social interactions, we found that identity information is highly represented in facial speech movements. In contrast to other non-rigid facial movements (e.g., emotional facial expressions), there is a strong link between auditory and visual modalities when processing speech movements (McGurk & MacDonald, 1976). A recent model of face and voice processing proposes that a person's voice and face are integrated in the representation of that person's identity (Campanella & Belin, 2007). Evidence supporting this model showed that human observers can match identities across video and audio recordings of spoken sentences (Kamachi, Hill, Lander, & Vatikiotis-Bateson, 2003). Moreover, facial speech movements not only enhance the comprehension of speech, but are also useful for face recognition (Rosenblum et al., 2002; Rosenblum, Johnson, & Saldaña, 1996). In line with these results, computational analyses of spatio-temporal characteristics in speech-related facial movements revealed that these movements provide sufficient information for person identification (Benedikt et al., 2010; Luettin et al., 1996). Our results confirmed previous findings by showing that sensitivity was highest in the social interaction context containing speech-related movements for both human and model observers. Taken together, we showed that more complex conversational and speech-related movements are performed less stereotypically than emotional facial expressions, and thus contain more identity information.

Recent neuroimaging studies have reported a dissociation between processing emotional versus neutral or speech-related (non-emotional) facial movements (Foley et al., 2012; Harris et al., 2014) suggesting separate processing routes for these different types of facial movements. If emotional facial expressions are processed separately from conversational facial expressions, they may also differ in the amount of identity information which is extracted during the processing. In line with this hypothesis, studies suggested that during processing of emotional facial movements, the brain further separates the representation of these facial expressions (Schyns et al., 2009; Smith et al., 2005). While these processing strategies may allow for fast adaptation to evolutionary salient emotional facial expressions (e.g., a fearful face indicates fast approaching danger), they may be sub-optimal to extract identity information. In contrast, studies investigating the perception of conversational facial expressions revealed that motion enhances their recognition (Cunningham & Wallraven, 2009; Kaulard et al., 2012), suggesting that the spatio-temporal information is extracted to interpret these facial movements. These findings indicate that identity information may also be extracted during the processing of conversational facial movements. If more identity information would be extracted during the processing of non-emotional communicative facial movements, the difference in sensitivity between model and human observers should be larger for the emotional context than for contexts containing social interactions. Although there was a slight trend indicating that differences in sensitivity between human and model observers were largest for the emotional context and smallest for the social interaction context, this trend was not significant. Our data thus do not support the hypothesis that the processing of emotional and more complex facial expressions differ in how much identity information is extracted.

3.6 Conclusion

Our present study reveals that the amount of identity information in facial motion varies with the type of facial movement. While emotional facial expressions may have evolved to optimally convey social signals (e.g., fast approaching danger), conversational facial movements contain information about the identity of a person, which may contribute to the representation of that person. From a theoretical viewpoint, this allows to bridge the gap between the fast interpretation of emotional facial expressions and the identity-specific processing of conversational and speech-related facial movements. A direct practical implication of these results is that functional magnetic resonance studies should be able to tease apart the brain structures that are specialized for processing identity information in facial movements (see O'Toole et al., 2002 for a discussion). Further, the facial motion capture method we employed reveals the dynamics of different components of facial motion. For future research, such a technique allows for investigating what aspects of facial motion we use to identify a moving face. While identity cues from facial motion might not play a great role for healthy participants in everyday situations, studies suggest that facial motion is a helpful clue for participants with disorders of face perception such as prosopagnosia (Longmore & Tree, 2013). Taken together, our study shows how sensitive our perception of face identity is, and highlights distinct roles of different types of facial movements for face perception. Moreover, thanks to the high degree of stimulus control, our approach will allow us in the future to ask precise questions about how facial motion carries identity information, and how it is processed.

Acknowledgements

We would like to thank Dr. Stephan de la Rosa for advice on statistics; and Prof. Heinrich H. Bülthoff for support and promotion of this study. There was no conflict of interest.

3.7 References

Ambadar, Z., Schooler, J. W., & Cohn, J. F. (2005). Deciphering the enigmatic face the importance of facial dynamics in interpreting subtle facial expressions. Psychological Science, 16(5), 403–410.

Benedikt, L., Cosker, D., Rosin, P. L., & Marshall, D. (2010). Assessing the uniqueness and permanence of facial actions for use in biometric applications. Systems, Man and Cybernetics, Part a: Systems and Humans, IEEE Transactions on, 40(3), 449–460.

Bruce, V., & Young, A. (1986). Understanding face recognition. British Journal of Psychology, 77(3), 305–327.

Calder, A. J., & Young, A. W. (2005). Understanding the recognition of facial identity and facial expression. Nature Reviews Neuroscience, 6(8), 641–651. doi:10.1038/nrn1724

Campanella, S., & Belin, P. (2007). Integrating face and voice in person perception. Trends in Cognitive Sciences, 11(12), 535–543. doi:10.1016/j.tics.2007.10.001

Cunningham, D. W., & Wallraven, C. (2009). Dynamic information for the recognition of conversational expressions. Journal of Vision, 9(13), 7–7. doi:10.1167/9.13.7

Curio, C., Breidt, M., Kleiner, M., Vuong, Q. C., Giese, M. A., & Bülthoff, H. H. (2006). Semantic 3d motion retargeting for facial animation, 77–84.

Dobs, K., Bülthoff, I., Breidt, M., Vuong, Q. C., Curio, C., & Schultz, J. (2014). Quantifying Human Sensitivity to Spatio-Temporal Information in Dynamic Faces. Vision Research, 100, 78-87. doi:10.1016/j.visres.2014.04.009

Ekman, P. (1992). Are there basic emotions?

Ekman, P., & Friesen, W. V. (1976). Measuring facial movement. Environmental Psychology and Nonverbal Behavior, 1(1), 56–75.

Ekman, P., Sorenson, E. R., & Friesen, W. V. (1969). Pan-cultural elements in facial displays of emotion. Science.

Foley, E., Rippon, G., Thai, N. J., Longe, O., & Senior, C. (2012). Dynamic facial expressions evoke distinct activation in the face perception network: a connectivity analysis study. Journal of Cognitive Neuroscience, 24(2), 507–520.

Gill, D., Garrod, O. G. B., Jack, R. E., & Schyns, P. G. (2014). Facial Movements Strategically Camouflage Involuntary Social Signals of Face Morphology. Psychological Science. doi:10.1177/0956797614522274

Harris, R. J., Young, A. W., & Andrews, T. J. (2014). Dynamic stimuli demonstrate a categorical representation of facial expression in the amygdala. Neuropsychologia, 56, 47–52. doi:10.1016/j.neuropsychologia.2014.01.005

Haxby, J. V., Hoffman, E. A., & Gobbini, M. I. (2000). The distributed human neural system for face perception. Trends in Cognitive Sciences, 4(6), 223–233.

Hill, H., & Johnston, A. (2001). Categorizing sex and identity from the biological motion of faces. Current Biology, 11(11), 880–885.

Jack, R. E., Garrod, O. G., Yu, H., Caldara, R., & Schyns, P. G. (2012). Facial expressions of emotion are not culturally universal. Proceedings of the National Academy of Sciences, 109(19), 7241–7244.

doi:10.1073/pnas.1200155109/-/DCSupplemental/sm01.avi

Kamachi, M., Hill, H., Lander, K., & Vatikiotis-Bateson, E. (2003). "Putting the face to the voice": Matching identity across modality. Current Biology, 13(19), 1709–1714.

Kaulard, K., Cunningham, D. W., Bülthoff, H. H., & Wallraven, C. (2012). The MPI Facial Expression Database — A Validated Database of Emotional and Conversational Facial Expressions. PLoS ONE, 7(3), e32321. doi:10.1371/journal.pone.0032321.s002

Kleiner, M. (2010). Visual stimulus timing precision in psychtoolbox-3: tests, pitfalls and solutions (Vol. 39, p. 189). Presented at the Perception.

Knappmeyer, B., Thornton, I. M., & Bülthoff, H. H. (2003). The use of facial motion and facial form during the processing of identity. Vision Research, 43(18), 1921–1936. doi:10.1016/S0042-6989(03)00236-0

Lander, K., & Bruce, V. (2003). The role of motion in learning new faces. Visual Cognition, 10(8), 897–912.

Lander, K., & Chuang, L. (2005). Why are moving faces easier to recognize? Visual Cognition, 12(3), 429–442. doi:10.1080/13506280444000382

Lander, K., Chuang, L., & Wickham, L. (2006). Recognizing face identity from natural and morphed smiles. The Quarterly Journal of Experimental Psychology, 59(05), 801–808. doi:10.1080/17470210600576136

Longmore, C. A., & Tree, J. J. (2013). Motion as a cue to face recognition: Evidence from congenital prosopagnosia. Neuropsychologia, 1–12. doi:10.1016/j.neuropsychologia.2013.01.022

Luce, R. D. (1961). A choice theory analysis of similarity judgments. Psychometrika, 26(2), 151–163.

Luettin, J., Thacker, N. A., & Beet, S. W. (1996). Speaker identification by lipreading (Vol. 1, pp. 62–65). Presented at the Proceeding of Fourth International Conference on Spoken Language Processing. ICSLP '96, IEEE. doi:10.1109/ICSLP.1996.607030

Macmillan, N. A., & Creelman, C. D. (2004). Detection Theory. Psychology Press.

McGurk, H., & MacDonald, J. (1976). Hearing lips and seeing voices. Nature, 746–748. doi:10.1038/264746a0

Näsänen, R. (1999). Spatial frequency bandwidth used in the recognition of facial images. Vision Research, 39(23), 3824–3833.

O'Toole, A. J., Roark, D. A., & Abdi, H. (2002). Recognizing moving faces: A psychological and neural synthesis. Trends in Cognitive Sciences, 6(6), 261–266.

Rosenblum, L. D., Johnson, J. A., & Saldaña, H. M. (1996). Point-light facial displays enhance comprehension of speech in noise. Journal of Speech and Hearing Research, 39(6), 1159–1170.

Rosenblum, L. D., Yakel, D. A., Baseer, N., Panchal, A., Nodarse, B. C., & Niehus, R. P. (2002). Visual speech information for face recognition. Perception & Psychophysics, 64(2), 220–229.

Russell, J. A. (1994). Is there universal recognition of emotion from facial expressions? A review of the cross-cultural studies. Psychological Bulletin, 115(1), 102.

Sato, W., & Yoshikawa, S. (2007). Enhanced Experience of Emotional Arousal in Response to Dynamic Facial Expressions. Journal of Nonverbal Behavior, 31(2), 119–135. doi:10.1007/s10919-007-0025-7

Schweinberger, S. R., & Soukup, G. R. (1998). Asymmetric relationships among perceptions of facial identity, emotion, and facial speech. Journal of Experimental Psychology: Human Perception and

Performance, 24(6), 1748.

Schyns, P. G., Petro, L. S., & Smith, M. L. (2009). Transmission of Facial Expressions of Emotion Co-Evolved with Their Efficient Decoding in the Brain: Behavioral and Brain Evidence. PLoS ONE, 4(5), e5625. doi:10.1371/journal.pone.0005625.s008

Sekuler, A. B., Gaspar, C. M., Gold, J. M., & Bennett, P. J. (2004). Inversion Leads to Quantitative, Not Qualitative, Changes in Face Processing. Current Biology, 14(5), 391–396. doi:10.1016/j.cub.2004.02.028

Smith, M. L., Cottrell, G. W., Gosselin, F., & Schyns, P. G. (2005). Transmitting and Decoding Facial Expressions. Psychological Science, 16(3), 184–189. doi:10.1111/j.0956-7976.2005.00801.x

Snow, S. M., Lannen, G. J., O'Toole, A. J., & Abdi, H. (2002). Memory for moving faces: Effects of rigid and non-rigid motion. Journal of Vision, 2(7), 600–600. doi:10.1167/2.7.600

Tomkins, S. (1962). Affect Imagery Consciousness. Springer Publishing Company.

4 Attention to dynamic faces enhances the neural representation of expression and identity in the human face processing system

4.1 Abstract

Identity and facial expression of faces we interact with are represented as invariant and changeable features, respectively - what are the cortical mechanisms that allow us to selectively extract information about these two socially relevant cues? We had participants attend to either identity or expression of the same dynamic face stimuli and decoded concurrently measured fMRI activity to ask whether attention enhances the representation of identity and expression in dynamic face processing. Multivoxel pattern analyses revealed distinct neural codes for the two attentional tasks across early visual and face-sensitive areas. Importantly, we could reliably decode specific exemplars of expression and identity if the feature was attended. Thus, our findings suggest that attention enhances the representation of high-level facial features across multiple stages of the visual face processing system.

4.2 Introduction

When seeing a friend, we may need to selectively extract identity information from his face to recognize him and information about his facial expression to interpret his mood. Current models of face perception distinguish between these features as invariant (i.e., facial identity) and changeable (i.e., facial expression) aspects of faces which are predominantly processed in distinct cortical areas (Haxby, Hoffman, & Gobbini, 2000). The core system comprises three areas: the occipital face area (OFA) in the inferior occipital gyrus (Allison et al., 1994; Gauthier & Logothetis, 2000); the posterior part of the superior temporal sulcus (STS) (Allison, Puce, & McCarthy, 2000; Narumoto, Okada, Sadato, Fukui, & Yonekura, 2001); and the fusiform face area (FFA) in the lateral fusiform gyrus (Gauthier & Logothetis, 2000; Kanwisher, McDermott, & Chun, 1997; Sergent, Ohta, & MacDonald, 1992). While OFA is thought to be involved in early perception of facial features (Pitcher, Walsh, & Duchaine, 2011), FFA and STS are thought to process invariant and changeable aspects of faces, respectively (Haxby et al., 2000). Several lines of evidence supporting the distributed model of face perception come from studies investigating neural correlates of attention in face processing (Furey et al., 2006; O'Craven, Downing, & Kanwisher, 1999; Wojciulik, Kanwisher, & Driver,

1998). Functional magnetic resonance imaging (fMRI) studies have suggested that selective attention to changeable versus invariant features of faces specifically increases activity in areas processing these features (Hoffman & Haxby, 2000; Narumoto et al., 2001). If so, why does neural activity in these areas increase with attention and what are the underlying mechanisms of attentional modulation in face processing?

Attention represents a powerful and ecological mechanism allowing us to selectively extract information about features of a face, such as identity or expression. Neurophysiological and neuroimaging studies have shown that selective attention to features of a stimulus increases responses of neurons and BOLD signal in early visual areas, indicating enhanced the representation of the attended features (Corbetta, Miezin, Dobmeyer, Shulman, & Petersen, 1990; Martinez-Trujillo & Treue, 2004; McAdams & Maunsell, 2000; Motter, 1994). Although feature-based attention has been widely investigated in the area of low-level visual processing, much less is known about its mechanism in high-level processing. For face processing, higher activity in face-sensitive areas may reflect the enhanced representation of facial features as required by the attentional task. Indeed, a recent fMRI study reported enhanced representation of individual faces in voxels preferring the attended face (Gratton, Sreenivasan, Silver, & D'Esposito, 2013). If attention to facial features may enhance the representation of facial features in the face processing network, we expect an improved representation of identity and expression when attending to these socially relevant facial features.

Although the neural correlates of face perception have been widely investigated, previous studies have mainly focused on static faces. However, faces occurring in real-life are in motion and observers are highly sensitive to the spatio-temporal information conveyed by dynamic faces (Curio et al., 2006; Dobs et al., 2014). Compared to static faces, this dynamic information facilitates the perception of expressions (Ambadar, Schooler, & Cohn, 2005; Cunningham & Wallraven, 2009; Kaulard, Cunningham, Bülthoff, & Wallraven, 2012; Krumhuber, Kappas, & Manstead, 2013), and even of identity (Hill & Johnston, 2001; Knappmeyer, Thornton, & Bülthoff, 2003; Lander & Bruce, 2003; Lander & Chuang, 2005; O'Toole, Roark, & Abdi, 2002). Although static face stimuli elicit activation in areas processing changeable aspect of faces, this effect is assumed to result from implied motion (Fairhall & Ishai, 2007; Haxby, Hoffman, & Gobbini, 2002). Indeed, response within the face processing network is stronger to dynamic than to static faces (Fox, Iaria, & Barton, 2009; Sato, Kochiyama, Yoshikawa,

Naito, & Matsumura, 2004; Schultz & Pilz, 2009; Schultz, Brockhaus, Bulthoff, & Pilz, 2013). Moreover, multivariate analyses of fMRI data in monkeys suggest that distinct neural codes represent static and dynamic facial expressions (Furl, Hadj-Bouziane, Liu, Averbeck, & Ungerleider, 2012). Thus, dynamic stimuli would offer a more suitable means of investigating which cortical areas of the face processing network represent identity or expression information.

In this study, we investigated how attention modulates the neural representation of expression and identity along early and late stages of dynamic face processing. To this end, we conducted an fMRI experiment in which participants attended to either the expression or identity of the same dynamic faces, while their brain activity was measured. Disentangling these two attentional tasks requires a tight control of dynamic face stimuli that has been previously impossible. Here, we animated two avatar faces with motion-recorded facial expressions (angry or happy) and used these animations as stimuli. To investigate the neural correlates of feature-based attention, we adapted a recent approach that was successful in decoding direction and color of a visual stimulus (T. Liu, Hospadaruk, Zhu, & Gardner, 2011). Using multivoxel pattern analysis, we were able to reliably decode which facial feature (i.e., expression or identity) was attended to across multiple cortical areas. Analyses of classifier weights and response magnitude revealed that cortical areas could be dissociated by which feature elicited greater activity, consistent with previous findings for static faces. Classifier analyses showed that representation of identity and expression were enhanced with attention. Moreover, identity was widely represented across face-sensitive areas and attentional tasks suggesting that identity information may be used to process expression during dynamic face processing. Our results are the first to find an enhanced representation of high-level facial features with attention across multiple stages of the visual face processing system.

4.3 Methods

Participants

Six observers (two female; mean age: 32 years) from the RIKEN Brain Science Institute volunteered as participants for the experiment. All observers were right-handed and had normal or corrected-to-normal vision. All participants provided informed written consent prior to the experiment. The psychophysical and neuroimaging experiments were approved by the Ethic Committee of the RIKEN Brain Science Institute.

Stimuli and display

We used videos displaying female avatar faces animated with previously recorded dynamic facial expressions (Fig. 1A) as stimuli. The animation procedure was as follows. First, two facial expressions (angry, happy) were motion-recorded from one non-professional female actor. Both facial expressions were 2 s long and started from a neutral expression which proceeded to the target expression. Second, two avatar faces (ID1, ID2) were designed in Poser 8 (SmithMicro, Inc., Watsonville, CA, USA). Third, both avatar faces were animated by each of the motion-captured facial expressions (for details about the motion-retargeting procedure see (Curio et al., 2006; Dobs et al., 2014). Finally, the four animations were rendered as Quicktime movies of 2 s duration (450 x 600 pixels, 30 frames at 60 Hz) in 3ds Max 2012 (Autodesk, Inc., San Rafael, CA, USA). The same methods were repeated for creating distractors: two additional identities and two additional expressions served to create morphs of the target faces or target expressions (see below the design and procedure section).

Stimuli were presented using MGL (http://justingardner.net/mgl) and Matlab (version R2010a; The MathWorks, Inc., Natick, MA, USA). Images were backprojected on a projection screen (Stewart Filmscreen, Torrance, CA, USA; 28.3 x 20.0 cm size, 800 x 600 pixel resolution, 60 Hz refresh rate) located inside the scanner at 50 cm viewing distance from the participant. Animation stimuli were scaled to a size of approximately 9° x 12° and positioned such that the tip of the avatar's nose was located at the center of the screen.

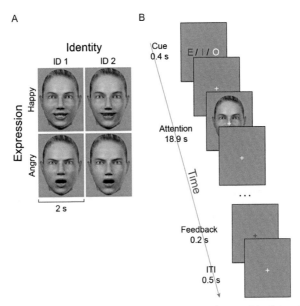

Figure 1. Experimental stimuli and procedure. (A) Representative frames of the four animation videos (duration: 2 s each) used as stimuli in the experiment. (B) The trial procedure of the attention experiment. ITI, Intertrial interval.

Design and procedure

To manipulate participants' attention to either expression or identity, we directed their attention to expression or identity while watching streams of dynamic face stimuli. Participants were instructed to either attend the expression (letter 'E') or identity (letter 'I'), or to not pay attention to anything specific (letter '0'), as indicated by a cue presented for 0.3 s at the beginning of each trial (Fig. 1B). In each trial, which lasted 20 s, the same animation stimuli (e.g., ID1 animated by facial expression happy) was repeatedly shown eight times. A fixation cross was constantly presented and participants maintained fixation over the duration of each trial, which was monitored by eye tracker (see below). Each scanning run consisted of eight attention-to-identity, eight attention-to-expression and four no-attention trials for a total of 20 trials (400 s/run). The order of trials was pseudorandomized such that the first trial in a run was always a no-attention trial and each trial type was combined with each of the four stimuli equally often (each stimulus was shown twice in an attention-to-identity trial, twice in an attention-to-expression trial and once in a no-attention trial). We included no-attention trials to have a baseline in which participants attended to neither expression nor identity.

To test whether participants successfully attended the cued feature, we had them perform a change detection task on either expression or identity of the dynamic face stimuli. Within each run, one-fourth of attention trials (two attention-to-identity and two attention-to-expression trials, randomized order) contained changes (referred to as "change trials" below). We did not include changes on all trials because we wanted to have clean trials for fMRI analysis in which neither changes in stimuli nor motor responses could drive differences in neural activity. However, participants treated all trials as change trials as they were not aware in advance about whether a trial contained changes. In change trials, one to four of the eight stimuli in a trial were randomly replaced by distractor stimuli which were slightly modified in either expression or identity. The distractor stimuli were created by linearly morphing the avatar's face into another facial identity (i.e., change in identity) or by linearly morphing the avatar's motion into another dynamic facial expression (i.e., change in expression). We used two distractor identities (ID3 and ID4) and two distractor expressions (disgust and surprise) as morph targets which differed from those used as stimuli. The amount of stimulus change (i.e., the morph level) was controlled via a one-up, two-down staircase procedure to maintain performance at an intermediate level (75% correct). Participants had to respond within the presentation of a distractor stimulus (2 s) or up to 500 ms afterwards for the response to count as a hit, which caused a decrease in the morph level of the subsequent distractor stimulus (i.e., a smaller change); two subsequent misses or false alarms caused an increase in the morph level (i.e., a larger change). At the end of each trial, participants were given feedback on their performance via a 0.2 s change in the color of the fixation cross. Green indicated that all changes in the cued feature were detected and correctly rejected in the uncued feature, yellow indicated partial detection or rejection, and red indicated that responses contained only false alarms or misses.

Before the first scanning session, participants practiced the change detection task for at least one hour in a psychophysics laboratory until they reached a stable performance level (75% accuracy) across all four stimuli and attentional tasks. The psychophysical training was identical to the scanning experiment with the exception that no-attention trials were not included in the training. To ensure that participants clearly discriminated the two identities (ID1 from ID2) and the two expressions (angry from happy), we further asked them to label each of the four stimuli before the start of the scanning experiment.

Participants completed a minimum of 16 and up to 20 runs in the scanner divided in two sessions on separate days. Imaging data acquired during change trials were discarded from the analysis to avoid confounds with motor response or effects due to perceptual differences across trials. As each run started with a no-attention trial, we further discarded no-attention trials from the analysis to eliminate effects of transient T1 signal change commonly seen at the start of an fMRI run.

Behavioral data analysis

For each subject, we calculated mean sensitivity (d' value) and reaction time for the two attentional tasks (i.e., attention-to-expression, attention-to-identity) and the two attended stimuli (i.e., angry and happy) from the responses of all test trials. To test for differences in task difficulty between the experimental conditions, we submitted the sensitivity and reaction time data to a 2 attentional tasks x 2 stimuli repeated-measures ANOVA.

Eye tracking

To ensure that participants maintained accurate fixations, we monitored eye position using an infrared eye tracker (Eyelink 1000, SR research, 500Hz) during psychophysical training and scanning. These data were available for at least one scanning session per subject. Eye position data were analyzed offline and evaluated for stability of fixation using custom Matlab code. For one scanning session of each subject, we baseline-corrected eye tracking data in each run and calculated the median horizontal and vertical eye position across runs for the experimental conditions. In particular, we assessed whether eye position differed across experimental conditions using t-tests (separately for vertical and horizontal eye position) and Hotelling's T2 test (for both vertical and horizontal eye position).

Magnetic resonance imaging protocol

Scanning was performed at RIKEN Brain Science Institute (Wako, Japan) on a 4 Tesla Varian Unity Inova whole-body MR system (now Agilent Technologies, Santa Clara, CA, USA) equipped with a head gradient system. In a separate scanning session, a T1-weighted high-resolution 3D anatomical image (MPRAGE; TR, 13 ms; TI, 500 ms; TE, 7 ms; flip angle, 11; voxel size, 1x1x1 mm; matrix, 256x256x180) and T2*-weighted (TR, 13 ms; TE, 7 ms; flip angle, 11; voxel size, 1x1x1 mm; matrix, 256x256x180) fast, low-angle shot sequence were acquired from each subject with a birdcage radio frequency (RF) coil. The T1-weighted volume was then divided by the T2*-weighted volume to form the reference high-resolution 3D anatomical volume (Van de Moortele et al., 2009). The functional images were acquired using an echo-planar imaging (EPI) pulse sequence with two shots per image (TR, 1.5 s; TE, 30 ms; flip angle, 55; voxel size, 3x3x3 mm; matrix, 64x64; interleaved) and a 16-channel LifeService coil. Scans were collected in 34 axial slices at an angle approximately perpendicular to the calcarine sulcus. To align the functional data to the high-resolution anatomical images, we also acquired a T1-weighted anatomical image with the same slice prescription as the functional scans at the beginning of each scanning session.

Preprocessing

Preprocessing contained various steps to reduce artifacts. Respiration and heartbeat was recorded during scanning and used to attenuate physiological signals in the imaging time series by estimating and correcting physiological fluctuation in k space (Hu et al., 1995). We then corrected the functional data for potential head movements (Nestares & Heeger, 2000) and linearly detrended and high-pass filtered the data at 0.01 Hz.

Task localizer scan

At the beginning of each scanning session, we ran a "task localizer" scan to identify voxels responding to the experimental task and visual stimuli. We designed the task localizer as a block design which allowed us to run correlation analyses on the data. Participants were instructed to perform the same task as they were trained outside the scanner. The trial procedure was identical to the training except for that the trial duration was shorter (i.e., a stimulus within a trial was repeated four instead of eight times). The trial duration was thus reduced to 10 s, and task trials were alternated with a 10 s blank (no task) fixation period. One-fourth of these localizer trials were change trials containing one or two stimuli changes. Participants performed two scanning runs with ten task on-off alternations in each run.

To identify voxels modulated by the experimental paradigm, we performed a Fourier-based analysis on the task localizer data. We first concatenated the functional data of the two task localizer runs. For each voxel, we then computed the correlation (coherence) between the measured time series and the best-fitting sinusoid at the stimulus-alternation frequency (Heeger, Boynton, Demb, Seidemann, & Newsome, 1999; T. Liu et al., 2011). The coherence value represents a measure of how well the activity of each voxel can be explained by the experimental task. We sorted all voxels in each area in descending order according to their coherence value and selected voxels with a coherence value of 0.4 or higher. However, to keep the number of selected voxels balanced, we restricted the number of voxels in each area to a lower bound of 20 (i.e., selecting also voxels with coherence < 0.4 if necessary) and an upper bound of 150 voxels. Note that the data used to compute these coherence values were acquired in different runs than the data used for the main analysis.

Retinotopic mapping

In a separate scanning session, we mapped early visual cortex for each subject using standard methodology (Gardner, Merriam, Movshon, & Heeger, 2008). Participants were shown 10-12 runs of high-contrast sliding radial checkerboard patterns as expanding and contracting rings (two runs each) or clockwise and counterclockwise rotating wedges (three to four runs each) for 10.5 cycles of 24 s. Averaged voxel time courses were Fourier transformed and the phase of voxel response at stimulus frequency was displayed on flattened maps of the cortical surface. We defined borders between visual areas as phase reversals in a polar angle map of the visual field. For each subject, we defined the following early visual areas across hemispheres: V1, V2, V3, hV4, and hMT+. The definition of hV4 was a hemifield representation anterior to V3v (Wandell, Dumoulin, & Brewer, 2007).

Face localizer scan

For each subject, we defined face-sensitive areas in the occipital and temporal lobe based on a separate category localizer scan. The fMRI protocol for this localizer slightly differed from the other scans. Functional images were acquired using an EPI pulse sequence (TR, 1.07 s; TE, 25 ms; flip angle, 63.5; voxel size, 3x3x3 mm; matrix, 64x64; interleaved) and a 16-channel LifeServices coil. Scans were collected in 27 axial slices aligned with the inferior surface of the occipital and temporal lobes. In a block design, participants viewed six runs of phase scrambled gray-scale images belonging to nine different categories (human face, building, human body, car, flower, fruit or vegetable, musical instrument, scrambled and gray images) while performing a 1-back repetition detection task. Each run contained 50 randomized blocks (block duration 12.9 s) of different image categories (image display time, 0.75 s; size, 14° x 14°) for a total run duration of about ten minutes. Based on these imaging data, we defined human face-sensitive areas as clusters of voxels which responded more to human faces than to buildings (FDR-corrected $p < 0.05$). Note that although participants viewed only static images of faces, we found voxels in bilateral superior temporal sulcus responding more to faces than buildings for all participants. Finally, we compared face-sensitive areas obtained from the face localizer with voxels active in the task localizer to ensure that voxels in these areas were also activated by our experimental task. We then used the combined activation (i.e., the union of activation across localizers) to define face-sensitive areas. We localized OFA in the lateral inferior occipital gyrus (Gauthier et al., 2000), FFA in the mid-fusiform gyrus (Kanwisher et al., 1997; McCarthy, Puce, Gore, & Allison, 2003), and STS in the posterior part of the superior temporal sulcus. Since studies reported differences in face processing mechanisms across hemispheres (Kanwisher et al., 1997; Rossion, Joyce, Cottrell, & Tarr, 2003), we defined face-sensitive areas separately for each hemisphere to assess differences in activation between the two hemispheres.

fMRI data analysis

BOLD response instances for classifier and amplitude analyses
We computed a BOLD "response instance" for each cortical area representing the pattern of BOLD activity in response to each trial. These response instances consisted of

a scalar value for each voxel indicating its trial activity as average percent signal change in the trial. We obtained response instances as follows. First, we converted the data of each run to percent signal change by dividing the time course of each voxel by its mean signal over a run. Second, we calculated the single-trial fMRI response for all voxels in a cortical area by averaging their response in a 3-21 s time window after trial onset. The time window was shifted by 3 s to compensate for the hemodynamic delay. Third, from these scalar responses, we selected responses of voxels which fulfilled the coherence criterion (see above) to form a response instance. Finally, for each subject, we concatenated response instances across both sessions. Collections of these instances were then used to run classifiers analyses and to calculate the mean response amplitude for both attentional tasks and stimulus parameters.

Multivoxel pattern classification

To assess whether there were different patterns of response to different conditions, we used binary linear discriminant analyses. For each subject, we built linear classifiers using Fisher's linear discriminant analysis (T. Liu et al., 2011). Briefly, to predict the class of a novel instance, Fisher's linear discriminant projects the instance onto a weight vector and compares the resulting scalar to a bias point. This weight vector is constructed based on the means of the two classes of instances used to build the classifier. The absolute classifier weight assigned to a voxel in the construction of a classifier indicates the contribution of this voxel to the two decisional classes such that non-informative voxels (e.g., with similar responses across classes) obtain small weights. Importantly, Fisher's linear discriminant assigns classifier weights such that positive weights indicate higher mean activity in the first class (in our case, attention-to-expression), while negative weights indicate higher mean activity in the second class (in our case, attention-to-identity).

To evaluate the accuracy of the classifier performance, we performed a leave-one-run-out cross-validation procedure and permutation analyses. For each subject, a training set was constructed by removing response instances from one run, and using the remaining runs to train a classifier. Response instances of the left-out run were then provided as input to the classifier and classification outputs were recorded. This procedure was repeated for each run of the data. The classifier accuracy was calculated as the number of correct classifications over the total number of classifications (across instances and left-out runs). We obtained the mean classifier accuracy by averaging accuracy values across participants and performed permutation analyses to assess the statistical significance of this mean classifier accuracy. To this end, for each subject, we again performed leave-one-run-out cross-validation but randomly reassigned the labels of the training data. We repeated this procedure 1000 times and averaged the accuracy values across participants to compute a distribution of expected mean classifier accuracies. The statistical significance was then calculated as the proportion of the permutation distribution that was greater than or equal to the observed mean classifier accuracy (Nichols & Holmes, 2002).

Classifier weight analysis

To determine if there were mean differences in the pattern of responses evoked by different conditions, we analyzed the weights assigned by linear classifiers. For each subject, we constructed a classifier based on all response instances across runs and read out the corresponding weights assigned by the classifier. We then calculated the mean weights across participants for each area to assess whether voxels showed higher response in the first (i.e., positive mean weights) or the second (i.e., negative mean weights) condition. To assess whether these mean weights were statistically different from chance, we performed permutation analyses to obtain the chance level of each area. To that end, for each subject, we constructed a classifier based on randomized labels and calculated the mean weights for 1000 repetitions. The mean of the distribution across permutations and participants was taken as the expected chance level mean weight. We then compared the observed mean weight for each area with its expected chance level via t-tests.

Response amplitude analysis

To assess whether differences in pattern of responses to experimental conditions were due to difference in mean activity, we analyzed the mean response amplitude in cortical areas. For each area, we calculated the mean response amplitude by concatenating data across response instances and runs and averaging across voxels. Response instances were the same as used for the classifier analyses. To assess the direction of difference in response amplitude between conditions, we subtracted the response amplitude observed in the attention-to-identity task from the response observed in the attention-to-expression task and compared this difference to zero using t-tests.

4.4 Results

Behavioral results

In this experiment, participants were cued to selectively attend either the expression or the identity of dynamic faces (Fig. 1). To assess whether participants successfully attended the cued feature, we introduced change trials in one fourth of attentional trials. In these trials, slight changes in expression or identity were presented and participants were instructed to press a button as soon as they detected a change in the cued feature. We controlled the magnitude of changes for each feature via an adaptive staircase procedure to ensure that task difficulty was matched across the attentional tasks.

Analysis of the behavioral performance in change trials showed that participants were able to selectively attend the cued feature (Fig. 2A). Sensitivity measured as d' was high in both tasks (attention-to-expression: d' mean and SEM = 2.21 ± 0.24, attention-to-identity: d' mean and SEM = 2.10 ± 0.16). A two-way repeated-measures ANOVA revealed no difference between sensitivity to changes in attention-to-identity and attention-to-expression tasks ($F(1,5)$ = 0.12, p = 0.73), suggesting equal sensitivity to the two attentional tasks. Furthermore, no difference in sensitivity between the two expressions (i.e., angry versus happy) or the two identities was found ($F(1,5)$ = 0.13, p = 0.73), suggesting that task difficulty was successfully matched across stimuli.

Despite matching difficulty between tasks, we did find some differences in reaction times between tasks (Fig. 2B). Participants took longer to detect a change in expression (mean reaction time: 1.71 ± 0.14 s) than a change in identity (mean reaction time: 1.20 ± 0.18 s) as confirmed by a two-way repeated measures ANOVA ($F(1,5)$ = 100.43, p < 0.0001). However, no difference in reaction time was observed between the two expressions or the two identities ($F(1,5)$ = 3.78, p = 0.07). This finding points out a potential confound of attentional effects that might be due to longer attention or higher mental load in the attention-to-expression condition.

Finally, analysis of eye tracking data showed that participants maintained stable fixation during all conditions. The median horizontal and vertical eye position during a trial did not depend on the attentional task (horizontal eye position: $t(5) = 1.75$, $p > 0.14$; vertical eye position: $t(5) = -0.16$, $p > 0.88$) and there was no difference in eye position across attentional tasks ($F(2,4) = 3.1$, $p > 0.15$, Hotelling's T2 test). Moreover, no pairwise comparison of median vertical and horizontal eye position revealed significant differences between facial expressions (angry versus happy: $p > 0.12$) or identities (ID1 versus ID2: $p > = 0.27$) across attentional tasks. Accordingly, in both attentional tasks, participants' eye position did not depend on the type of expression ($F(2,4) < = 3.64$, $p > = 0.13$) or identity ($F(2,4) < = 2.08$, $p > = 0.24$). Thus, we can exclude the contribution of eye movements to the attentional effects.

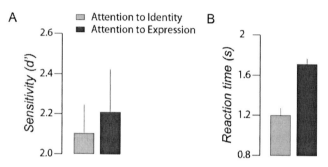

Figure 2. Behavioral results obtained from change trials. (A) Mean sensitivity (d') and (B) mean reaction times in test trials for the two attentional tasks. Error bars indicate + 1 SEM across participants (n = 6).

Multivoxel pattern classification: attentional task

We first asked whether any visual cortical areas showed different patterns of responses during the different attentional tasks (Fig. 3A). For each subject, we selected voxels based on how active they were in an independent task localizer and constructed classifiers for each area (see Methods). We then calculated the mean classifier accuracy for each area by averaging across participants. We used permutation tests to evaluate whether the mean accuracy was greater than chance. Classifier performance was above chance in early visual and all face-sensitive areas ($p < 0.01$) suggesting that all areas showed different patterns for attention to expression and identity.

We next examined whether the ability to decode the attentional task was due to simple increases or decreases in response across whole regions of cortex (Fig. 3B). The weights assigned to each voxel by the classifier not only indicate how informative a voxel is for the classification but further indicate in which condition a voxel shows higher response (e.g., attention-to-expression versus attention-to-identity). For each subject, we thus calculated the average of all classifier weights in an area and averaged these weights across participants for each area. We then compared the mean weight of each area to its expected chance level obtained from permutation analysis.

We found that visual areas were dissociated by their mean response to the conditions. For early visual areas, the mean weights were negative (V1: $t(5) = -2.53$, $p < 0.05$; V2: $t(5) = -2.52$, $p < 0.05$; V3: $t(5) = -2.50$, $p < 0.05$) or showed a negative trend (hV4: $t(5) = -1.97$, $p < 0.10$) indicating that voxels in these areas responded more in trials involving attention-to-identity than attention-to-expression. In contrast, the mean weights in the motion-processing area hMT+ were greater than chance level ($t(5) = 2.67$; $p < 0.05$) suggesting that voxels showed greater responses when attending to expression than to identity. For face-sensitive areas, we found differences between hemispheres: Weights in areas in the right hemisphere were not different from chance (rOFA: $t(5) = -1.20$, $p > 0.1$; rFFA: $t(5) = -1.36$, $p > 0.1$; rSTS: $t(5) = 1.39$, $p > 0.1$). However, voxels in areas in the left hemisphere had negative weights in the occipital and temporal lobe (lOFA: $t(5) = -2.51$, $p < 0.05$; lFFA: $t(5) = -2.04$, $p < 0.05$), while weights of voxels in the left superior temporal sulcus were positive (lSTS: $t(5) = 6.57$, $p < 0.01$).

These findings suggest that all areas were modulated by the attentional task but areas were dissociated by which task revealed greater response. Attending to identity recruited early visual areas and face-sensitive areas involved in discriminating invariant aspects of faces (lOFA, lFFA). In contrast, areas involved in the processing of changeable aspects of faces (hMT+, lSTS) showed enhanced activity when attending to expression. Interestingly, areas involved in later stages of face processing showed a distinction between the left and the right hemisphere such that areas in the left hemisphere showed differences in overall activity between tasks, while right hemisphere areas did not. However, right hemisphere areas still showed discriminative patterns for attention to expression and identity.

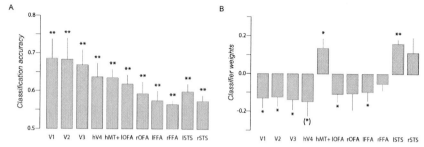

Figure 3. Multivoxel pattern analysis results for the attentional task (attention-to-expression versus attention-to-identity). (A) Mean classifier accuracy for predicting the attended feature across participants (n = 6) at selected voxels (r2 > 0.4) for face-sensitive and early visual cortical areas. Chance performance is 0.5, corresponding to 50% correct. Asterisks indicate significance level obtained from permutation analyses (*: p < 0.05, **: p < 0.01). (B) Mean classifier weights (n = 6) at the same voxels. Positive weights indicate higher activity in attention-to-expression and negative weights indicate higher activity in attention-to-identity. Error bars indicate + 1 SEM across participants. Asterisks indicate significance level obtained from comparing to expected chance level (*: p < 0.05, **: p < 0.01, (*): p < 0.10).

Average response across attentional tasks

Finally, we asked whether cortical areas showed differences in average response amplitude between the attentional tasks as suggested by the classifier weight analysis. For each subject, we selected the same voxels as for the multivoxel pattern analysis. Within each area, we then calculated the mean percent signal change across voxels separated for the attentional tasks. To assess whether there were mean differences in response amplitude, we subtracted the response amplitude in the attention-to-identity task from the response in the attention-to-expression task and compared the difference to zero using t-tests. A positive difference value represents higher response in attention-to-expression versus attention-to-identity trials; and vice versa for negative values. Differences close to zero indicate that there was no difference in overall response amplitude between the two attentional tasks. Note that this analysis is similar to the classifier weight analysis (see Fig. 3B). However, we assume the average response analysis to be less sensitive than the classifier weight analysis as all voxels contribute similarly to the average response. In contrast, only voxels which are informative for the classification are regarded in the classifier weight analysis (i.e., non-informative voxels have weights close to zeros and thus do not contribute).

Analysis of the average response across areas confirmed the results obtained from the classifier weight analysis (Fig. 4). Attending to expression and identity differently modulated the average response in visual areas. While voxels in early visual areas showed larger response amplitudes for attention-to-identity than attention-to-expression (V1: $t(5) = -2.59$, $p < 0.05$; V2: $t(5) = -2.98$, $p < 0.05$; V3: $t(5) = -2.85$, $p < 0.05$; hV4: $t(5) = -1.99$, $p < 0.1$), the motion-processing area hMT+ showed the opposite effect ($t(5) = 2.88$; $p < 0.05$). This dissociation was less clear for areas involved in the later stages of face processing. As hypothesized, we found higher response amplitudes for attention-to-expression than for attention-to-identity in left STS ($t(5) = 5.33$, $p < 0.01$), but the same trend was not observed in right STS ($t(5) = 1.28$, $p > 0.1$). Furthermore, mean response amplitudes in ventral face-sensitive areas in the right hemisphere did not differ between attentional tasks (rOFA: $t(5) = -1.32$, $p > 0.1$; rFFA: $t(5) = -0.42$, $p > 0.1$). However, there was a marginal trend for ventral areas in the left hemisphere (lOFA: $t(5) = -1.92$, $p < 0.1$; lFFA: $t(5) = -1.55$, $p < 0.1$) suggesting that attending to identity yielded larger overall responses in these areas.

Because we found longer reaction times when participants had to detect changes in expression compared to identity, differences in activity between the attentional tasks could be due to higher activation in this condition. However, this possibility seems unlikely given that we found no difference in behavioral sensitivity across attentional conditions. In addition, for most of the areas, mean responses were larger when attending to identity than when attending to expression. The only exception were two areas involved in processing changeable aspects of faces, namely hMT+ and left STS, for which we predicted higher activity when attending to expression than when attending to identity.

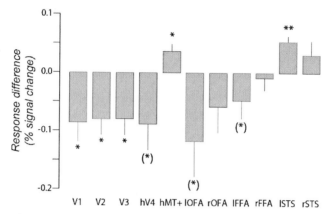

Figure 4. Results of the analysis of average responses across attentional tasks (attention-to-expression versus attention-to-identity). Mean response difference (n = 6) at selected voxels (r2 > 0.4) in face-sensitive and early visual cortical areas. Positive difference values indicate higher response amplitude in attention-to-expression and negative weights indicate higher response amplitude in attention-to-identity. Error bars indicate + 1 SEM across participants (n = 6). Asterisks conventions are the same as in Fig. 3.

Multivoxel pattern classification: representation of expression and identity

Next, we investigated which areas represent expression by assessing if the expression exemplar presented could be decoded from the data obtained in our areas of interest.We found that we could decode expression during attention to expression but not during attention to identity from data obtained in early visual and motion-processing areas (Fig. 5A). To reveal this, we constructed classifiers for each subject and each area and trained them on the two expressions (i.e., angry versus happy) separately for the attentional tasks (see Methods). We calculated the mean classifier accuracy for each area and both attentional tasks by averaging across participants. We used permutation tests to compare the observed classifier accuracy with the accuracy expected by chance. In the attention to expression condition, early visual cortex areas V1, V2, V3 and hV4 ($p < 0.01$, permutation-test), motion-processing area hMT+ ($p < 0.01$) and right STS ($p < 0.01$) showed distinctive patterns for the two expressions, suggesting that these areas represent expressions. However, when attending to identity, the pattern for both expressions did not differ in any of the areas (accuracy < 0.58, $p >= 0.07$). Thus, these results suggest that attention to expression is necessary to reliably represent that feature.

Next, we investigated which areas represent identity by assessing if the identity exemplar presented could be decoded from the data obtained in our areas of interest. We found that identity could be decoded from the data of multiple areas when attending that feature (Fig. 5B). We revealed this by training classifiers on the two different identities separately for both attentional tasks and compared the mean classifier performance to the corresponding permutation distribution. When attending to identity, classifiers using the data from early visual areas V1 ($p < 0.01$) and V3 ($p < 0.05$) and from face-sensitive areas in the bilateral occipital (lOFA, rOFA: $p < 0.05$), the bilateral ventral temporal lobe (lFFA, rFFA: $p < 0.05$) and the right STS ($p < 0.01$) could reliably decode the identity. When attending to expression, early visual cortex V1 ($p < 0.01$), right OFA and right STS still showed a discriminative pattern between identities ($p < 0.05$) suggesting that these areas represent identity irrespective of the attended feature. In addition, identity could be decoded during attention-to-expression from hV4 data. Compared to our results about decoding of expression exemplars, these results indicate that representation of identity is more distributed across visual areas, suggesting that identity information is also represented in areas processing expressions.

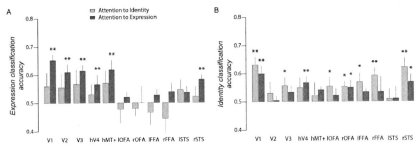

Figure 5. Multivoxel pattern analysis results for the representation of expression and identity. Mean classifier accuracy for decoding exemplars of expression (A) and identity (B), shown separately for the attentional tasks. Accuracy of 0.5 represents chance level. Error bars indicate + 1 SEM across participants (n = 6). Asterisks conventions are the same as in Fig. 3.

4.5 Discussion

We have shown that feature-based attention enhances the representation of high-level facial features, namely expression and identity of dynamic faces, across multiple stages of the visual processing hierarchy. First, multivoxel pattern analyses revealed that attending to the identity versus the expression of dynamic faces is reflected in task-specific neural patterns in early visual and face-sensitive areas. Importantly, these areas were dissociated by their response to the attentional tasks as revealed by classifier weight analysis. Attention to identity recruited early visual and face-sensitive areas involved in discriminating invariant aspects of faces, while attention to expression activated areas involved in processing changeable aspects. These results were confirmed by a univariate analysis showing that mean response amplitude discriminated which feature was attended in early visual areas, motion-processing area hMT+ and left STS. Finally, we demonstrated that feature-based attention modified the representation of expression and identity across the visual processing hierarchy. Multivoxel pattern classifiers in multiple areas could reliably decode the attended feature while decoding performance was at chance for the unattended feature. Compared to expression, we found that the representation of identity was more distributed across face-sensitive areas. Moreover, several areas (V1, hV4, right OFA and right STS) seem to represent identity when expression was attended suggesting that identity information may be processed more automatically and may be relevant in processing facial expressions. Together, our results suggest that the representations of identity and expression dynamically change with attention in the well studied face processing system.

Dissociation of cortical areas by their modulation with attention

Accumulating evidence suggests that attention modulates activity in the face processing system. Using static faces, several studies found decreased activity in face-selective areas when attention was directed away from faces towards different objects (Furey et al., 2006; O'Craven et al., 1999; Wojciulik et al., 1998). Several studies further investigated modulation of brain activity when directing attention to different features within static images of faces (Hoffman & Haxby, 2000; Narumoto et al., 2001; Sergent, Ohta, MacDonald, & Zuck, 1994; Winston, O'Doherty, & Dolan, 2003). In line with the proposed distributed model of face perception (Haxby et al., 2000), neuroimaging studies reported greater response in STS when attention was directed to changeable aspects (e.g., emotion, eye gaze) compared to the identity of static faces (Hoffman & Haxby, 2000; Narumoto et al., 2001; Winston et al., 2003). Our results confirm these findings in STS and extend them by showing that response in motion-processing area hMT+ is higher for attention to expression than attention to identity in dynamic face stimuli.

However, results are less clear for the ventral temporal face processing regions: While studies have shown greater response in OFA and FFA for attention to identity than attention to changeable aspects of faces (Hoffman & Haxby, 2000), contrary finding have also been reported (Ganel, Valyear, Goshen-Gottstein, & Goodale, 2005; Narumoto et al., 2001). These divergent results could be due to differences in task difficulty or physical differences in stimuli between the attentional tasks for the latter studies. To avoid these potential confounding factors in the present study, we carefully matched task difficulty and used identical stimuli for both attentional tasks, and found increased responses during attention to identity compared to attention to expression in OFA and FFA. In addition, areas in early stages of visual processing (V1-V3, hV4) showed stronger responses during attention to identity than for attention to expression, suggesting that representation of static features of faces (including the dynamic faces we used) is boosted during processing of identity. Overall, our results confirm that face-sensitive areas can be dissociated by their engagement during processing of changeable versus invariant aspects of dynamic faces as proposed by an influential model of face perception (Haxby et al., 2000), and extend previous findings by showing that attentional modulation occurs across early and late stages of visual face processing.

Interaction between expression and identity information

It is still under debate whether invariant and changeable aspects of faces are represented in anatomically distinct areas and to which extent both representations interact (Calder & Young, 2005; Ganel & Goshen-Gottstein, 2004). Two lines of evidence support an interaction between the processing of identity and expression.

First, behavioral (Schweinberger & Soukup, 1998; Schweinberger, Burton, & Kelly, 1999) and neuroimaging studies (Baseler, Harris, Young, & Andrews, 2014; Fox, Oruc, & Barton, 2008) found that variations in identity influence the processing of expressions. In our present data, we could only decode the expression presented when participants attended to expression, suggesting that representation of this feature was suppressed while extracting identity information. In contrast, identity could be decoded from the data of areas V1, OFA and right STS, irrespective of the attentional task. These results suggest that areas involved in processing low-level visual attributes of facial features and changeable aspects of faces process and represent identity information even when attention is directed to expression. Thus, our results are consistent with the hypothesis that identity information is used in areas processing changeable aspects of faces to compute expressions (Baseler et al., 2014; Ganel & Goshen-Gottstein, 2004; Schweinberger et al., 1999).

Second, fMRI studies using static faces have reported expression and identity information across face-sensitive areas using adaptation techniques (Fox et al., 2009; Winston, Henson, Fine-Goulden, & Dolan, 2004; Xu & Biederman, 2010) and multivariate pattern analysis (Nestor, Plaut, & Behrmann, 2011). In line with these results, we found identity information in STS, suggesting that identity is processed across face-sensitive areas. However, in contrast to previous studies which reported expression information in ventral temporal regions (Fox et al., 2009; Winston et al., 2004; Xu & Biederman, 2010), we could not decode expression in OFA or FFA. This finding suggests that expression information is selectively represented in areas involved in changeable aspects of faces. Why did our results differ from previously reported findings?

On the one hand, the absence of expression information could be due to differences in processing static versus dynamic faces. Several studies found increased activation of face-sensitive areas in response to dynamic versus static face stimuli (Fox et al., 2009; Schultz et al., 2013; Schultz & Pilz, 2009). A recent neuroimaging study in monkeys suggested that distinct neural codes might be used for dynamic and static representations of expressions (Furl et al., 2012). Connectivity analysis further revealed differences in coupling between face-sensitive areas for static versus dynamic faces (Foley, Rippon, Thai, Longe, & Senior, 2012). Thus, dynamic faces might engage neural structures in ventral face areas which do not carry expression information. This could be an important addition to the literature given that dynamic face stimuli are closer to face stimuli encountered in real life.

On the other hand, the fact that we could not decode expression from OFA and FFA data could be due to the lack of idiosyncratic motion dynamics in our facial expression stimuli. Indeed, behavioral studies have found that observers can extract identity information from facial motion (Hill & Johnston, 2001; Knappmeyer et al., 2003; Lander & Chuang, 2005; Lander, Chuang, & Wickham, 2006). Here, we applied the same motion to both identities, which eliminates any individual differences in the way an expression can be performed. Perhaps there really are no representations of expression in ventral face-processing areas, but this can only be revealed using highly controlled stimuli such as the ones we used in the current study. Thus, individual dynamics may be necessary to extract unique expressions useful for computing identity.

The representation of identity and expression information in OFA and hMT+

The area OFA is thought to represent facial components prior to subsequent processing of complex facial features in higher face-selective cortical regions (Fox et al., 2009; Large, Cavina-Pratesi, Vilis, & Culham, 2008; Pitcher et al., 2011; Rotshtein, Henson, Treves, Driver, & Dolan, 2004). In line with these findings, we could decode identity information from OFA data irrespective of the attentional task. However, we did not find expression information in OFA, suggesting that motion information may be extracted in different visual areas. A potential candidate region could be hMT+. We found that we could decode the expression presented from hMT+ data, when participants attended to expression, which is consistent with the role of this region in processing motion information for faces (O'Toole et al., 2002). In contrast, we could not find evidence that identity information is represented in this area, which suggests that hMT+ is not involved in processing static identity information. In the future, however, it would be interesting to investigate whether information about idiosyncratic motion patterns across different identities could be revealed in OFA or hMT+.

Effects of feature-based attention in early visual cortex

While most studies investigating neural correlates of facial feature processing focused on high-level face-sensitive areas, much less is known about how earlier visual areas (i.e., V1-V3, hV4) are involved in face perception. Here, we found that the representation of identity and expression was enhanced by attention not only in face-selective, but also in early stages of the visual processing hierarchy. For example, expression could be decoded in V1-V3 and hV4 when attending to expression but not when attending to identity. This result suggests that feature-based attention acts as a mechanism by which the representations of facial features get enhanced already in early visual processing stages. While selective attention has been shown to enhance neural responses to low-level features in early visual cortex (Reynolds & Chelazzi, 2004), we are the first to report early visual cortex representations of the high-level face features expression and identity in a feature-based attentional task. Furthermore, the finding that we could decode identity and expression in early visual cortex, despite the careful match of low-level stimulus attributes, is in line with a recent study which indicates that V1 is modulated by top-down influences during face processing (Petro, Smith, Schyns, & Muckli, 2013). In summary, our results suggest that attention may act via a unitary principle of selective enhancement of responses along all stages of the visual hierarchy, and that high-level face features may be represented in early visual cortex via top-down influences.

Attentional modulation of identity and expression representation

Our results suggest that feature-based attention can selectively modify the representation of identity and expression across multiple stages of visual face processing. Why might this be the case? Studies investigating attentional modulation of low-level features suggested that attention enhances responses (McAdams & Maunsell, 2000; Motter, 1994) and sharpens the tuning of neurons to these features (Martinez-Trujillo & Treue, 2004). In line with these results, a recent study reported that selective attention to individual faces can enhance responses in voxels representing the attended face (Gratton et al., 2013). Here, we found that in a highly ecological task, namely attending to the expression versus the identity of faces, representations of exemplars within these features were enhanced with attention. Thus, our results suggest that the representation of facial features in cortical areas might be dynamic rather than static, and that attention might act as a mechanism to boost the representations of these high-level facial features.

Acknowledgements

This work was supported in part by the Japan Society for the Promoting of Science (JSPS) Fellowship PE1251. We thank Kenji Haruhana and the Support Unit for Functional Magnetic Resonance Imaging at RIKEN Brain Science Institute for assistance conducting functional imaging experiments and Toshiko Ikari for administrative assistance. We also thank Topi Tanskanen for collecting and providing neural data for the localizer and Prof. Heinrich H. Bülthoff for support. There was no conflict of interest.

4.6 References

Allison, T., Ginter, H., McCarthy, G., Nobre, A. C., Puce, A., Luby, M., & Spencer, D. D. (1994). Face recognition in human extrastriate cortex. Journal of Neurophysiology, 71, 821–821.

Allison, T., Puce, A., & McCarthy, G. (2000). Social perception from visual cues: role of the STS region. Trends in Cognitive Sciences, 4(7), 267–278.

Ambadar, Z., Schooler, J. W., & Cohn, J. F. (2005). Deciphering the enigmatic face the importance of facial dynamics in interpreting subtle facial expressions. Psychological Science, 16(5), 403–410.

Baseler, H. A., Harris, R. J., Young, A. W., & Andrews, T. J. (2014). Neural Responses to Expression and Gaze in the Posterior Superior Temporal Sulcus Interact with Facial Identity. Cerebral Cortex, 24(3), 737–744. doi:10.1093/cercor/bhs360

Calder, A. J., & Young, A. W. (2005). Understanding the recognition of facial identity and facial expression. Nature Reviews Neuroscience, 6(8), 641–651. doi:10.1038/nrn1724

Corbetta, M., Miezin, F. M., Dobmeyer, S., Shulman, G. L., & Petersen, S. E. (1990). Attentional modulation of neural processing of shape, color, and velocity in humans. Science, 248(4962), 1556–1559.

Cunningham, D. W., & Wallraven, C. (2009). Dynamic information for the recognition of conversational expressions. Journal of Vision, 9(13), 7–7. doi:10.1167/9.13.7

Curio, C., Breidt, M., Kleiner, M., Vuong, Q. C., Giese, M. A., & Bülthoff, H. H. (2006). Semantic 3d motion retargeting for facial animation, 77–84.

Dobs, K., Bülthoff, I., Breidt, M., Vuong, Q. C., Curio, C., & Schultz, J. (2014). Quantifying human sensitivity to spatio-temporal information in dynamic faces. Vision Research, 100, 78-87. doi:10.1016/j.visres.2014.04.009

Fairhall, S. L., & Ishai, A. (2007). Effective Connectivity within the Distributed Cortical Network for Face Perception. Cerebral Cortex, 17(10), 2400–2406. doi:10.1093/cercor/bhl148

Foley, E., Rippon, G., Thai, N. J., Longe, O., & Senior, C. (2012). Dynamic facial expressions evoke distinct activation in the face perception network: a connectivity analysis study. Journal of Cognitive Neuroscience, 24(2), 507–520.

Fox, C. J., Iaria, G., & Barton, J. J. S. (2009). Defining the face processing network: Optimization of the functional localizer in fMRI. Human Brain Mapping, 30(5), 1637–1651. doi:10.1002/hbm.20630

Fox, C. J., Oruc, I., & Barton, J. J. S. (2008). It doesn't matter how you feel. The facial identity aftereffect is invariant to changes in facial expression. Journal of Vision, 8(3), 11–11. doi:10.1167/8.3.11

Furey, M. L., Tanskanen, T., Beauchamp, M. S., Avikainen, S., Uutela, K., Hari, R., & Haxby, J. V. (2006). Dissociation of face-selective cortical responses by attention. Proceedings of the National Academy of Sciences, 103(4), 1065–1070.

Furl, N., Hadj-Bouziane, F., Liu, N., Averbeck, B. B., & Ungerleider, L. G. (2012). Dynamic and Static Facial Expressions Decoded from Motion-Sensitive Areas in the Macaque Monkey. Journal of Neuroscience, 32(45), 15952–15962. doi:10.1523/JNEUROSCI.1992-12.2012

Ganel, T., & Goshen-Gottstein, Y. (2004). Effects of Familiarity on the Perceptual Integrality of the Identity and Expression of Faces: The Parallel-Route Hypothesis Revisited. Journal of Experimental Psychology: Human Perception and Performance, 30(3), 583–597. doi:10.1037/0096-1523.30.3.583

Ganel, T., Valyear, K. F., Goshen-Gottstein, Y., & Goodale, M. A. (2005). The involvement of the "fusiform face area" in processing facial expression. Neuropsychologia, 43(11), 1645–1654. doi:10.1016/j.neuropsychologia.2005.01.012

Gardner, J. L., Merriam, E. P., Movshon, J. A., & Heeger, D. J. (2008). Maps of Visual Space in Human Occipital Cortex Are Retinotopic, Not Spatiotopic. Journal of Neuroscience, 28(15), 3988–3999. doi:10.1523/JNEUROSCI.5476-07.2008

Gauthier, I., & Logothetis, N. K. (2000). Is face recognition not so unique after all? Cognitive Neuropsychology, 17(1-3), 125–142.

Gauthier, I., Tarr, M. J., Moylan, J., Skudlarski, P., Gore, J. C., & Anderson, A. W. (2000). The fusiform "face area" is part of a network that processes faces at the individual level. Journal of Cognitive Neuroscience, 12(3), 495–504.

Gratton, C., Sreenivasan, K. K., Silver, M. A., & D'Esposito, M. (2013). Attention Selectively Modifies the Representation of Individual Faces in the Human Brain. Journal of Neuroscience, 33(16), 6979–6989. doi:10.1523/JNEUROSCI.4142-12.2013

Haxby, J. V., Hoffman, E. A., & Gobbini, M. I. (2000). The distributed human neural system for face perception. Trends in Cognitive Sciences, 4(6), 223–233.

Haxby, J. V., Hoffman, E. A., & Gobbini, M. I. (2002). Human neural systems for face recognition and social communication. Biological Psychiatry, 51(1), 59–67.

Heeger, D. J., Boynton, G. M., Demb, J. B., Seidemann, E., & Newsome, W. T. (1999). Motion opponency in visual cortex. The Journal of Neuroscience, 19(16), 7162–7174.

Hill, H., & Johnston, A. (2001). Categorizing sex and identity from the biological motion of faces. Current Biology, 11(11), 880–885.

Hoffman, E. A., & Haxby, J. V. (2000). Distinct representations of eye gaze and identity in the distributed human neural system for face perception. Nature Neuroscience, 3(1), 80–84.

Hu, X., Le, T. H., Parrish, T., & Erhard, P. (1995). Retrospective estimation and correction of physiological fluctuation in functional MRI. Magnetic Resonance in Medicine, 34 (2), 201-212.

Kanwisher, N., McDermott, J., & Chun, M. M. (1997). The fusiform face area: a module in human extrastriate cortex specialized for face perception. The Journal of Neuroscience, 17(11), 4302–4311.

Kaulard, K., Cunningham, D. W., Bülthoff, H. H., & Wallraven, C. (2012). The MPI Facial Expression Database — A Validated Database of Emotional and Conversational Facial Expressions. PLoS ONE, 7(3), e32321. doi:10.1371/journal.pone.0032321.s002

Knappmeyer, B., Thornton, I. M., & Bülthoff, H. H. (2003). The use of facial motion and facial form during the processing of identity. Vision Research, 43(18), 1921–1936. doi:10.1016/S0042-6989(03)00236-0

Krumhuber, E. G., Kappas, A., & Manstead, A. S. R. (2013). Effects of Dynamic Aspects of Facial Expressions: A Review. Emotion Review, 5(1), 41–46. doi:10.1177/1754073912451349

Lander, K., & Bruce, V. (2003). The role of motion in learning new faces. Visual Cognition, 10(8), 897–912.

Lander, K., & Chuang, L. (2005). Why are moving faces easier to recognize? Visual Cognition, 12(3), 429–442. doi:10.1080/13506280444000382

Lander, K., Chuang, L., & Wickham, L. (2006). Recognizing face identity from natural and morphed smiles.

The Quarterly Journal of Experimental Psychology, 59(05), 801–808. doi:10.1080/17470210600576136

Large, M.-E., Cavina-Pratesi, C., Vilis, T., & Culham, J. C. (2008). The neural correlates of change detection in the face perception network. Neuropsychologia, 46(8), 2169–2176. doi:10.1016/j.neuropsychologia.2008.02.027

Liu, T., Hospadaruk, L., Zhu, D. C., & Gardner, J. L. (2011). Feature-Specific Attentional Priority Signals in Human Cortex. Journal of Neuroscience, 31(12), 4484–4495. doi:10.1523/JNEUROSCI.5745-10.2011

Martinez-Trujillo, J. C., & Treue, S. (2004). Feature-Based Attention Increases the Selectivity of Population Responses in Primate Visual Cortex. Current Biology, 14(9), 744–751. doi:10.1016/j.cub.2004.04.028

McAdams, C. J., & Maunsell, J. H. (2000). Attention to both space and feature modulates neuronal responses in macaque area V4. Journal of Neurophysiology, 83(3), 1751–1755.

McCarthy, G., Puce, A., Gore, J. C., & Allison, T. (2003). Face-specific processing in the human fusiform gyrus. Journal of Cognitive Neuroscience, 9(5). doi:10.1126/science.272.5268.1665

Motter, B. C. (1994). Neural correlates of feature selective memory and pop-out in extrastriate area V4. The Journal of Neuroscience, 14(4), 2190–2199.

Narumoto, J., Okada, T., Sadato, N., Fukui, K., & Yonekura, Y. (2001). Attention to emotion modulates fMRI activity in human right superior temporal sulcus. Cognitive Brain Research, 12(2), 225–231.

Nestares, O., & Heeger, D. J. (2000). Robust multiresolution alignment of MRI brain volumes. Magnetic Resonance in Medicine, 43(5), 705–715.

Nestor, A., Plaut, D. C., & Behrmann, M. (2011). Unraveling the distributed neural code of facial identity through spatiotemporal pattern analysis. Proceedings of the National Academy of Sciences, 108(24), 9998–10003. doi:10.1073/pnas.1102433108/-/DCSupplemental/pnas.201102433SI.pdf

Nichols, T. E., & Holmes, A. P. (2002). Nonparametric permutation tests for functional neuroimaging: a primer with examples. Human Brain Mapping, 15(1), 1–25.

O'Craven, K. M., Downing, P. E., & Kanwisher, N. (1999). fMRI evidence for objects as the units of attentional selection. Nature, 401(6753), 584–587.

O'Toole, A. J., Roark, D. A., & Abdi, H. (2002). Recognizing moving faces: A psychological and neural synthesis. Trends in Cognitive Sciences, 6(6), 261–266.

Petro, L. S., Smith, F. W., Schyns, P. G., & Muckli, L. (2013). Decoding face categories in diagnostic subregions of primary visual cortex. European Journal of Neuroscience, 37(7), 1130–1139. doi:10.1111/ejn.12129

Pitcher, D., Walsh, V., & Duchaine, B. (2011). The role of the occipital face area in the cortical face perception network. Experimental Brain Research, 209(4), 481–493. doi:10.1007/s00221-011-2579-1

Reynolds, J. H., & Chelazzi, L. (2004). Attentional modulation of visual processing. Annual Review of Neuroscience, 27, 611–647.

Rossion, B., Joyce, C. A., Cottrell, G. W., & Tarr, M. J. (2003). Early lateralization and orientation tuning for face, word, and object processing in the visual cortex. NeuroImage, 20(3), 1609–1624. doi:10.1016/j.neuroimage.2003.07.010

Rotshtein, P., Henson, R. N. A., Treves, A., Driver, J., & Dolan, R. J. (2004). Morphing Marilyn into Maggie dissociates physical and identity face representations in the brain. Nature Neuroscience, 8(1), 107–113. doi:10.1038/nn1370

Sato, W., Kochiyama, T., Yoshikawa, S., Naito, E., & Matsumura, M. (2004). Enhanced neural activity in response to dynamic facial expressions of emotion: an fMRI study. Cognitive Brain Research, 20(1), 81–91. doi:10.1016/j.cogbrainres.2004.01.008

Schultz, J., & Pilz, K. S. (2009). Natural facial motion enhances cortical responses to faces. Experimental Brain Research, 194(3), 465–475. doi:10.1007/s00221-009-1721-9

Schultz, J., Brockhaus, M., Bulthoff, H. H., & Pilz, K. S. (2013). What the Human Brain Likes About Facial Motion. Cerebral Cortex, 23(5), 1167–1178. doi:10.1093/cercor/bhs106

Schweinberger, S. R., & Soukup, G. R. (1998). Asymmetric relationships among perceptions of facial identity, emotion, and facial speech. Journal of Experimental Psychology: Human Perception and Performance, 24(6), 1748.

Schweinberger, S. R., Burton, A. M., & Kelly, S. W. (1999). Asymmetric dependencies in perceiving identity and emotion: Experiments with morphed faces. Perception & Psychophysics, 61(6), 1102–1115.

Sergent, J., Ohta, S., & MacDonald, B. (1992). Functional neuroanatomy of face and object processing. A positron emission tomography study. Brain, 115(1), 15–36.

Sergent, J., Ohta, S., MacDonald, B., & Zuck, E. (1994). Segregated processing of facial identity and emotion in the human brain: A pet study. Visual Cognition, 1(2), 349–369. doi:10.1080/13506289408402305

Van de Moortele, P.-F., Auerbach, E. J., Olman, C., Yacoub, E., Uğurbil, K., & Moeller, S. (2009). T1 weighted brain images at 7 Tesla unbiased for Proton Density, T2 contrast and RF coil receive B1 sensitivity with simultaneous vessel visualization. NeuroImage, 46(2), 432–446. doi:10.1016/j.neuroimage.2009.02.009

Wandell, B. A., Dumoulin, S. O., & Brewer, A. A. (2007). Visual Field Maps in Human Cortex. Neuron, 56(2), 366–383. doi:10.1016/j.neuron.2007.10.012

Winston, J. S., Henson, R. N. A., Fine-Goulden, M. R., & Dolan, R. J. (2004). fMRI-Adaptation Reveals Dissociable Neural Representations of Identity and Expression in Face Perception. Journal of Neurophysiology, 92(3), 1830–1839. doi:10.1152/jn.00155.2004

Winston, J. S., O'Doherty, J., & Dolan, R. J. (2003). Common and distinct neural responses during direct and incidental processing of multiple facial emotions. NeuroImage, 20(1), 84–97. doi:10.1016/S1053-8119(03)00303-3

Wojciulik, E., Kanwisher, N., & Driver, J. (1998). Covert visual attention modulates face-specific activity in the human fusiform gyrus: fMRI study. Journal of Neurophysiology, 79(3), 1574–1578.

Xu, X., & Biederman, I. (2010). Loci of the release from fMRI adaptation for changes in facial expression, identity, and viewpoint. Journal of Vision, 10(14), 36–36. doi:10.1167/10.14.36